Bravo, Young Buffs!

Bravo, Young Buffs!
The Recollections of an Officer of the 31st (Huntingdonshire) Regiment of Foot During the Peninsular War

George B. L'Estrange

With a Short Historical Record of the 31st or Huntingdonshire Regiment of Foot by Richard Cannon

Bravo, Young Buffs!
The Recollections of an Officer of the 31st (Huntingdonshire) Regiment of Foot During the Peninsular War
by George B. L'Estrange
With a Short Historical Record of the 31st or Huntingdonshire Regiment of Foot
by Richard Cannon

FIRST EDITION

Leonaur is an imprint of Oakpast Ltd
Copyright in this form © 2016 Oakpast Ltd

ISBN: 978-1-78282-515-9 (hardcover)
ISBN: 978-1-78282-516-6 (softcover)

http://www.leonaur.com

Publisher's Notes

The views expressed in this book are not necessarily those of the publisher.

Contents

Off to the Peninsula!	7
The Great Escape	20
The Battle of Vittoria	33
In the Pyrenees	44
Crossing the Nive	56
The Advance into France	67
Towards Toulouse	74
Anecdotes of War	87
Appendix	101
The 31st or Huntingdonshire Regiment of Foot During the Napoleonic Period	121

CHAPTER 1

Off to the Peninsula!

Two generations have now nearly passed away, (1874), since the great duke brought to a conclusion the glorious Peninsular War, placed Great Britain at the head of the nations of the world, and secured to his country a peace which lasted for thirty-nine years. It was my fortune to have taken a part, though a humble one, in those memorable campaigns, having joined my regiment, the 31st, when in winter quarters after the disastrous retreat from Burgos, November 1812, the siege of which Lord Wellington was unable to maintain. The greater part of the heroes who figured in those battles, and went through those interesting campaigns, have passed away; for years I have not met an old Peninsular officer, to talk over and remind me of scenes so long gone by, nor have I for a long period been able to meet a man with whom I could *"fight our battles o'er again, or again to slay our slain."* Though many books have been written on this very prolific subject, there may, however, probably be some anecdotes which will not be read without interest by a generous public, but which I feel must create a deep interest in the many members of my own family, as well as those whose names I shall take the liberty of introducing into these memoirs.

I read my original manuscript to one or two friends, on whose judgment and good taste I could rely; they urged me to proceed, but I had made up my mind the other way. I trust I have now apologised and accounted to my numerous friends for what I cannot flatter myself was a great disappointment, and I hope they will accept it as such. Though late, I shall now endeavour to redeem myself and restore my name to their good opinion, by publishing, as it may be convenient to me to produce them, some short sketches or "Scraps from Recollection," of a prolonged and not uneventful life.

I shall therefore commence with my departure for the Peninsula, in company of a cousin of my own, who was a hero in every sense of the word, and wound up a very glorious career by his death on the field of Waterloo, in the year 1815, *viz.* Major Edmund L'Estrange, of the 71st Highlanders, Light Infantry.

On the 1st of November, 1812, a splendid fleet of upwards of 300 sail of transports, with their men-of-war to convoy them to Lisbon, lay at Spithead, on board of which were embarked a large reinforcement of recruits to supply the vacancies in Lord Wellington's army, in which were detachments for most of the regiments then in Spain, and also the Household Brigade of Cavalry going out to him for the first time. My father's regiment, the King's County Militia, having volunteered for foreign service from Ireland, lay at Portsmouth, and as upwards of 100 of them had volunteered for the 31st Regiment, the second battalion being with the army in Spain. His Royal Highness the Duke of York presented me with a commission in that regiment, without purchase. These volunteers I marched up from Portsmouth to Ashford, in Kent, to undergo their preliminary drilling, and I must confess they were a set of wild Irishmen, whom I had some trouble and difficulty in coaxing along the march of several days. They were unarmed, but ready notwithstanding for any row that might turn up.

My father having given me a good horse, I rode at their head, and hit upon an expedient which I found very successful, which was to play Irish tunes for them on the flute, at which I was no great proficient, but they stepped along cheerily to their native country airs, and I joined with them all in safety at Ashford. They did not, however, remain long there, but were soon equipped with their uniform, had "Brown Bess" placed in their hands, and in a very short time we were on our return march to Portsmouth, to embark in the above fleet for the Peninsula. I took the precaution of embarking them the instant we arrived at Portsmouth, and we found ourselves on board a heavy-sailing transport brig, marked "*A 90*," which was a great relief to my mind, with my wild countrymen. I found on board "*A 90*" several detachments for other regiments, all under the command of Major Jessop, of the 44th Regiment, a splendid officer, a perfect gentleman, particularly handsome, and a capital good fellow. I regret to say I have never met him since to thank him for all his kindness to me, a young officer of fifteen years of age.

The sun rose bright on the morning of the next day, though it was November; and I have a perfect recollection of the splendid scene before me when I came early on deck, a brisk breeze from the north-

SIR GEORGE ON HORSEBACK, PLAYING THE FLUTE, AT THE HEAD OF THE IRISH VOLUNTEERS.

ward, and the Blue Peter flying at every mast-head. I was standing on the deck, looking with delight at everything around me, and anticipating the glories of a campaign with the "Great Duke," when a boat rowed alongside, and I was much surprised to hear my name asked for. I looked down, and saw a young man, who, immediately he heard I was on board, stepped on the quarter-deck, and said, "Don't you know me, George?"

I was not long in recognising my cousin Edmund, and said, "Where in the world have you dropped from? I thought you were a prisoner in France?"

"So I was," said he, "but I have made my escape; arrived in London yesterday morning; had an interview with his Royal Highness the Duke of York, related the particulars of my escape, and informed him that my great ambition was at once to rejoin my general, Sir Denis Pack, to whose staff I belong. His Royal Highness told me that there was a fleet lying at Spithead, waiting for a fair wind, in which was an officer of the name, and I might possibly overtake it before it sailed. I came down by the mail last night, and here I am; by-the-bye," said he, "I have not a farthing of money; can you help me?"

I said, "I have 120 dollars, and you shall certainly have the half of them."

In less time than I write the signal-gun for sailing was fired, and we, with a spanking breeze behind us, were under weigh, with our heads towards the Needles. The Isle of Wight and the Needles were rapidly passed under a bright sun, and as the evening closed in and darkened, a heavy cloud rose up towards the west, betokening a change in both wind and weather, which was soon realized, and as the night closed in in darkness, and almost blackness, we found ourselves in a gale of wind and a fearful sea. It fell to my lot to be on the midnight watch for the first time, and when I got up on deck in utter darkness, for we were not allowed to use lights, I felt a little dismayed.

There evidently was great risk of collision, and we could occasionally hear the roll of the drum in some vessel towering on the top of a wave, almost over our heads, of which nothing could be discovered but a dark mass, which we might at any moment come in contact with, and it would have been utter destruction had we struck it. We, however, escaped the dangers of this awful night; and when the day broke, of this numerous and gallant fleet, there was scarcely one sail in sight; but we frequently saw the black horses of the Household Brigade floating past us, thrown overboard, the victims of this tremendous storm.

It was nearly a fortnight before we sighted the shores of Portugal, and the scattered fleet dropped into the Tagus, at Lisbon, one at a time, and it was a considerable time before the last of them arrived at their destination. I began to be a pretty good sailor by this time, and I recollect coming off the morning watch, at eight o'clock, with a good appetite for my breakfast, and rushing across the cabin, where my comrades were pitching into it. In the dusk I did not perceive that the skipper was down below, and the trapdoor open, when I suddenly disappeared into those dark regions, an awful fall, which might have broken my neck. I was, however, speedily hauled up, and having escaped with some severe bruises, was soon endeavouring to appease my appetite on the unsavoury fare that usually accompanies breakfast on board such a transport as the "*A 90.*"

The *désagrémens* of the voyage rapidly disappeared when we saw the lateen sails of the Tagus boats, and were boarded by a Portuguese pilot. Everything was new and interesting to me, and it was with supreme delight that I passed by the fort of Belem and found myself in the calm and golden waters of the Tagus. Our detachment was soon landed and marched to their quarters; Edmund and I proceeded to Lisbon to secure our billets, and I was rejoiced to find that my loan to my cousin had fructified on the voyage to the sum of 200 dollars, the results of sundry games of chance with the other officers on board.

We were soon installed in our new billets, and proceeded to view the beauties and filth of Lisbon; our rations were served out, and I made my first essay in the culinary art by endeavouring to turn them into something resembling soup, but it was a very bad imitation, and I was not sorry to find that Edmund had several friends and acquaintances, some of whom asked us to dinner. Amongst the rest General Beresford, afterwards Lord Beresford, who was at Lisbon for the recovery from the wound he had received at the Battle of Albuera, had us frequently to dinner: he had known Edmund when a prisoner in South America, and my family in Ireland, and was the first Beresford I had become acquainted with, though I afterwards became more closely connected with some of this noble and distinguished family, of whom more hereafter.

I also met here Colonel Hardinge, afterwards Lord Hardinge, and D'Urban, afterwards Sir Benjamin D'Urban, and heard all the news from the army, which excited my youthful imagination, and I was only anxious to be off to join my regiment. This, however, I was unable to accomplish until nearly the end of the year 1812, but I amused myself very well in Lisbon, went to see all the sights there and at Cintra, and escaped many an "*aqua vai*" by a miracle as I returned from evening parties, operas, &c.; the opera here being open, to which was attached a gambling-house, to relieve the young officers sent out from England of their Crusadé Nuovos and Douros.

There was a celebrated and very handsome lady at the opera at that time, of the name of Brunét, and a Portuguese gentleman, of the name of Bandiera, seemed particularly struck with her, and as he sat in the stage-box, whenever she approached near enough he exclaimed "*Multa buoneta Brunét*." I should not, however, say anything disparaging of this gentleman, as he afterwards invited me to some of the splendid banquets he was in the habit of giving. Preparatory to going up the country it became necessary that I should procure means of locomotion, so accordingly one morning I repaired to the Rosio, where was held the market for horses, mules, &c., and I was not long in closing a bargain for a very tight little black English pony, for which I paid 100 dollars, and a long-legged ugly mule that I got for eighty.

Equipped with a pair of panniers covered with cow-hide, in which I placed all my worldly goods, having invested in a country pack-saddle over which the panniers were thrown across, a stretcher about six feet long, and a small hair mattress and a pair of blankets which sat on the mule's back between the panniers; having also invested in an English saddle and bridle for my pony, and a voluminous camlet cloak which nearly covered myself and horse, I felt myself prepared to meet the world in arms, and to drive the French Army beyond the Pyrenees, which fact we eventually accomplished.

Edmund had been on the look-out for some party proceeding to join Sir Rowland Hill's division, who would undertake the charge of a youth of my calibre in that direction. Two officers, of higher rank, in the 66th Regiment, then forming a provisional battalion with the 31st, one being a major the other a captain—I recollect their names but do not wish to give them—declined to be bothered with my company on my small pony, which probably could not keep up with them—and most likely they were right. My recruits from the King's County Militia had already started under command of other officers, and I only retained one of them—a quiet and thoroughly honest fellow, of the name of Tim Ferry (I shall have to record his death hereafter). But he soon discovered that a detachment of the 5th Dragoon Guards, under the command of Captain Sibthorp, afterwards the celebrated and eccentric member for Lincoln, was about to proceed to the front, his lieutenant being Richard Falkiner, who had two brothers, officers in my father's regiment: they most cheerfully undertook the charge.

I was not very well got up for a campaign, having no canteen; but my mule was soon equipped with pack-saddle; the cow-hide panniers, containing all my goods and chattels, were soon packed up, thrown across him, my bedding, &c., in the centre, the little black pony accoutred with camlet cloak in front of the saddle, and so I took a cordial and affectionate leave of Edmund, and commenced my journey to join, Tim being in charge of the baggage. But I forgot to mention that I had brought out a single-barrelled gun from England, of which we shall have more to say presently.

During our voyage out Edmund had frequently amused me with the account of his marvellous escapes from the fortress of Verdun and the dungeons of Bitche. They naturally made a deep impression on me, and I have a perfect recollection of many of the interesting circumstances and adventures that befell him. I have reason to know that there is extant the account of these escapes, written by himself. Since his death I have made many endeavours to recover them. The late General Brotherton told me that he had seen them, that he believed they were in Yorkshire, and that he would try to get them; in this he was not successful. But I think I have got a clue, and nearly run them to earth in Fifeshire; and if I get them they shall certainly appear, (these appear at the end of this book). Had he not fallen at Waterloo he would certainly have published them himself, for they were full of interest. He used to describe to me the amusements of the British officers on parole at Verdun; how they got up plays and balls.

At one of the latter he went disguised as a young French lady; his very fair complexion, his slight, rather small figure, and his perfect knowledge of French, favouring the deception. He succeeded so well that his particular friend Beamish, of the 31st, also a prisoner, did not suspect him in the least. He danced several times with him, and, in fact, became desperately smitten; followed him out into the street when the dance was over; was beside himself with joy in fancying he had gained the affections of the pretty French girl; and proceeding a little too far in his attentions, discovered his mistake. Exclaiming in his rich Irish brogue, "Arrah! What's the maning of this?" Edmund burst into loud laughter, and Beamish had to endure the chaffing of his brother prisoners for a long period.

Edmund, meantime, was pining to escape, for "he was sick of captive thrall." He meditated day and night how he could effect it, longing to rejoin the army that was prosecuting the war in the Peninsula, and to get back to his general, Pack. Nothing would induce him to break his parole, and he committed some trivial offence, for which he was placed in close arrest. He managed, however, one morning to get as far as the gates, close to which lived the woman that sold him milk. She discovered him at once, when he immediately confessed what he was about, threw himself on her generosity, and said it was a matter of life or death to him. She proved faithful. A waggon laden with hay was passing the gate; the woman engaged the sentry in conversation, directing his attention in a different direction, and he passed out of the gate at the opposite side of the waggon. He was free.

Beamish also managed to scale the walls, and by, I suppose, some preconcerted arrangement, they found each other in a small wood near Verdun, where they laid *perdu* till night.

I must have started with my friends of the 5th Dragoon Guards about the 20th of December, 1812. Our first three or four days' marching were not very interesting. I had sent my friend Tim with the baggage and my pony, and taking my gun on my shoulder I took across the country in the hope of having some shooting—a sort of steeplechase—in the direction which the detachment had taken. I cannot say that I was very successful; but on the day before Christmas I was so fortunate as to knock down three snipes, two of them at one shot, and they were a very acceptable addition to our Christmas dinner at Santarem, where we halted for that solemn day, and my two cavalry friends enjoyed this addition to our Christmas-day's fare of rations.

At Santarem I heard that the surgeon of our regiment, the celebrated and well-known Maurice Quil, who has since been immortalised in the genial pages of my friend Charles Lever, whose loss we now deplore, was stationed on sick leave; I therefore found out his billet, and went to call upon him. He came out to his door, and having explained to him who I was, he said, "Is it a nephew of Colonel L'Estrange you are?"

"Yes," says I.

"Ah, then, it's many the good dinner he gave me!"

I thought this sounded well, and fully expected an invitation from him in return. But no, Maurice Quil never asked me if I had "a mouth in my head;" and I made him my bow, and returned to the pretty good dinner my friends of the 5th Dragoons had prepared, with the addition of my three snipes.

The next morning we proceeded on our march, halting in one of the miserable Portuguese villages on the route to Abrantes. In one of these, arriving late and tired from my cross-country march, I repaired to the billet-master, who was the *alcaldé*, or *juez de pays* of the place, to ask for my billet. He kept a sort of a shop in the village, and I made known as well as I could the nature of my visit. I waited for a long time with great patience; and seeing that there was little chance of my procuring my billet, I fear I lost my temper, and, mustering up probably the only few words of Portuguese that I was acquainted with, I shouted out to him, "*Presto! Filho da Puta!*"

"*Filho da Puta vos mérsai!*" retorted the *alcaldé*, his yellow-brown face turning a ghastly yellow with rage, and he rushed about the shop, looking for a gun or some instrument to take vengeance on me. His wife in the meantime advanced to me, imploring me by her actions to leave the house to escape his rage, that he would think nothing of shooting me, which he probably might have done had not two or three English soldiers providentially entered the shop, which seemed to quell the *alcaldé's* rage, and I procured at length my billet.

We proceeded the following day on our march towards Abrantes. I still, in the vain hope of sport, went across country, got down to the banks of the Tagus, and on the last day of the year, when within about two miles of the town, I saw an orderly sergeant approaching me. When he reached me he asked if I were Ensign L'Estrange. I replied in the affirmative, and he told me that I was to proceed with as little delay as possible and report myself to the *commandant*. I lost little time in obeying this mandate; and, presenting myself at his office, found myself in the presence of a very rough-looking *militaire*, who showed me little civility, not even asking me to sit down.

This was Colonel Royal, who I afterwards learnt had risen from the ranks. He very shortly informed me that there was a detachment of the Guards delayed there two days by the illness of the officer in command, that it was an escort of twenty-five mules laden with dollars for headquarters, that I must take the command of them, and they were to march at daylight the next morning. The name of the officer who was taken ill was Lieutenant Simpson, of the Grenadier Guards, the same who afterwards commanded the army in the Crimea.

On the 1st January, 1813, as the dawn of day made objects tolerably distinct, a small detachment of the Grenadier Guards fell in in one of the streets of Abrantes. This was the detachment placed under my command, and I accordingly made my appearance at the appointed time. The admirable discipline and good conduct of the non-commissioned officers of the Guards is too well known to need any eulogy from me; but it was a fortunate circumstance for so young and inexperienced an officer as I was; and I can only say that I never had occasion to find fault with a single man, until I delivered them over into other hands at Frenada, then the headquarters of the British Army.

Then came a long line of small Spanish mules, all in good condition, with their long coats clipped closely under the pack-saddle, and various devices cut out on their shining coats; each of them carried two not very large but rather heavy boxes, for their contents were Spanish dollars, though not at all an overload for these useful animals. Three or four Spanish muleteers, in their picturesque dress—very fine-looking fellows—were in care of the mules; the whole being in charge of a Civil officer, an intelligent and gentlemanlike fellow, with whom I shortly became on very intimate terms. There was very little delay on the parade that dark and dismal and exceedingly cold morning. Taking the hint from the sergeant that all was ready I gave the word of command to march.

This was a sort of epoch in my life. I began to reflect, and it appeared to me a strange thing to find that I, who had never been supposed to be clever in taking care of my own money, should have such a vast sum suddenly thrust upon me, with the command of a body of men who could not be exceeded in the whole world. With thoughts of this nature, and looking back upon the kind and good friends I was so recklessly and suddenly separating from, I also began to think that I had neither knife, fork, spoon, nor any of the little necessaries so important to a young campaigner; and when we came to our first halt I was agreeably relieved by an invitation from the Civil officer to join him in a luncheon, a fine cold boiled chicken, which he produced out of his haversack: it needed no pressing to accept this hospitable invitation; and I even found the Spanish muleteers very kind in offering me part of their own messes. I suppose my youth, and evident want of preparation, had some effect of this sort, and I pursued my way not a little proud of the position I held, though I knew every step I was taking was in the wrong direction, Sir Rowland Hill's Division, to which I belonged, being far away to the south. (*General Rowland Hill* by Edwin Sidney & Alexander Innes Shand is also published by Leonaur).

We pursued our march through a desolate and devastated country until we arrived at Castello Branco, a city that had been the scene of one of the most bloody sieges of these warlike times. The town was a perfect ruin, and deserted by the inhabitants. We had twice crossed the Tagus, once on a bridge of boats, at Villa Vella; the surrounding country was of the most desolate and forbidding nature, the villages bearing the unmistakable marks of having been the seat of war, and the billets of the most wretched description, without furniture of any kind, admitting the cold and wind both above and below, and the weather most piercing cold. The only effect of all this upon me was a bad chilblain on my heel, which prevented my putting on a boot for some months.

After a long and weary march we at length arrived at Frenada, the headquarters. Lord Wellington was absent, and nobody knew where he was; but we afterwards found out that he had been at Cadiz, endeavouring to bring the Spaniards into more active co-operation with his British forces. I enjoyed a rest of a couple of days immensely, with a party of jovial fellows that I fell amongst, and at the end of that period received a route, or rather a sort of roving commission, to join the 2nd Division, Sir Rowland Hill's, which were in winter-quarters in the neighbourhood of Placentia. My route lay along the frontiers of Spain and Portugal. In some parts of it they had never seen a British soldier, and when I and my friend Tim, who was my only companion, presented ourselves at what we thought was our billet we were stared at with curiosity, and a certain suspicion which was far from pleasant, the Spanish peasantry at that time having become ferocious from all the miseries they had endured from the French invasion; and when I awoke in the morning from my rest, after a long day's march, I felt very grateful that my throat was not cut.

After a long and a most tedious and solitary march of several hundred miles, I at length turned up, to my great joy, in a village called Ceclavin, where the headquarters of General Byng's Brigade was stationed, and I found my regiment, the 31st, which I had been so long in search of.

I was received with open arms by the officers, who had given me up as lost, they having heard of my arrival in Lisbon in November, but received no further tidings. My uncle having been very popular when in command of the regiment ensured me this cordial reception. Captain Dowdall took me under his immediate protection, and ever acted until the end of the campaign as if he had been my father: his kindness I can never forget. The only fault I could find was that he treated me too kindly, and almost as a child, always insisting at our mess (for we had a mess) that I should be helped first to the pudding or pie that was provided, which I thought was rather derogatory to so experienced an officer. The morning after my arrival it was agreed that a Board should be held on my mule, whose shoulder had assumed an alarming proportion in size from the pressure of the pack-saddle, and Clifford, of the Buffs, an experienced and clever volunteer veterinary, came to the inspection. He shortly produced his lancet, and made a deep incision in the swelling.

I soon recovered from the fatigue of my long march; was excused from parade in consequence of not being able to put up the heel of my shoe, but was permitted to join the shooting-parties, headed by our gallant colonel, afterwards Sir Alexander Leith, with three or four of the captains, who were inveterate sportsmen. The colonel,, whom we all adored, and for whom we would have faced the black gentleman himself had he ordered us, was a rough Scotchman, who generally designated us as a parcel of "dom wavers," a term of reproach at that period in his country. Though I was only an ensign I was appointed to the light company then under the command of Captain Girdlestone, one of the finest fellows and best officers in the army. I was very proud of this appointment, particularly when I found that several of the volunteers from my father's Militia regiment were also included, and who ever afterwards went by the name of my pets. Alas! I fear that very few of them survived the two campaigns which immediately followed our joining the regiment.

We remained for some time at Ceclavin, proceeded thence to a small walled village called Galesteo, and from thence to Placentia, where we lay until the advance of the whole army was ordered, about the 15th of May. Whilst we lay at Galesteo, having formed the acquaintance of Lieutenant Stepney St. George, of the 66th regiment, then forming the 1st Provisional battalion with the 31st, of whom I shall have a good deal to relate hereafter, we became bosom friends and were constant companions in all the shooting excursions which were then the chief amusement of the British Army. It was in one of these parties that I was so fortunate as to knock down at a very long distance a splendid bustard. We brought him in in triumph to our quarters, and he regaled the mess for two days, Stepney St. George, of course, being invited to partake of him.

We never made very large bags, our ammunition being none of the best, of our own manufacture, and we never could discover the means of depriving the shot of the long tails that appertain to the home manufacture of this necessary article, and consequently our aim was not as deadly as if it came from our friend Mr. Walker's round tower at Chester, but we generally managed to bring in something, hares or rabbits, red-legged partridges or woodcocks, and a sort of small bustard that was very numerous in the district, but very difficult to get at. Nothing very particular occurred until the breaking up of the army, and our advance to Salamanca and Vittoria.

Chapter 2

The Great Escape

I observed in my first chapter that during our voyage to Lisbon and our stay there, my cousin, Edmund L'Estrange, gave me long and amusing accounts of his two escapes from the French prison of Verdun and from the fortress of Bitche; and that I had some hope of finding some notes he made at the time, but I have been disappointed. I must therefore trust to memory and some memoranda which I have fortunately preserved among the few relics I have of my first campaign. I have already mentioned that he, my cousin Edmund, got through the gates of Verdun unchallenged, and met his friend Beamish, his admirer at the ball as I before mentioned, at the place where the rendezvous was fixed in case they should both get safely away from the town.

They took the road towards the frontiers of the Netherlands. Fearing discovery, they hid themselves in the woods during the day, and only travelled at night; Beamish speaking only broken French, dared not attempt to purchase provisions or make inquiries as to the route. Edmund therefore, who fortunately spoke French like a native (a rare accomplishment in those days), performed the duty of foraging. I ought now to mention the change of costume of my cousin Edmund. During one of his foraging expeditions he made acquaintance with a French peasant girl, who we must suppose admired his pretty, girlish, and innocent face; but at all events, persuaded by the honeyed accents of one who had most probably kissed the blarney-stone, she sold him her *costume de fête*, or as we should say, her Sunday clothes, with which he retired to a neighbouring wood, and made himself up into the likeness of a French servant-girl.

He tied his own clothes up into a bundle and slung them over his shoulder, quite in the style of a French girl; not with a stick as an Irishman as he was would do, but with a thick red cotton handkerchief rolled into a rope; and to increase the resemblance he tied to the bundle a pair of wooden sabots, as if a girl going in her best clothes and shoes to service.

Approaching the frontiers of the Netherlands, Edmund and Beamish observed that *gendarmes* were much more frequently met; and as it would not have seemed natural that the girl should reply to any inquiry which might be made at any moment, Beamish decided to run the risk alone, and Edmund taking leave of his friend struck into the road to Furnes in the Western Flanders, from which town he intended to creep down to the shore, crossing the great salt-marshes between the town and the coast.

After several hair-breadth escapes, having been accosted and chucked under the chin, and on more than one occasion seized by the waist and kissed by an amorous *gendarme*; after having crept into a barn, and slept among the sheaves of corn, and been discovered by his loud snoring in the morning by two girls who entered to fetch their milking-pails and stools, and whom he amused with a long history of having run away from home because papa and mamma wished to marry *her* to a snuffy old village schoolmaster, the two girls took pity on her, and, indignant at the cruel usage of papa and mamma, gave her a large tartine of black bread and mackey, a kind of soft skim-milk cheese very common in the Netherlands, and a drink of new milk. They then put her on to a footpath leading to Furnes, to which place *he*, or rather *she*, said she was going to seek a place as "*bonne d'enfants.*"

However, it was night before Edmund arrived within view of the walls of Furnes, and, arriving at the gate, he found it was shut; and not venturing to go to the guard-house, he made up his mind to look out for a barn or stable in which to lie *perdu* until early morning. Creeping into a farmyard with the intention of ensconcing himself quietly in a barn or stable, the dogs of the farm set up a furious barking, and before he could retreat a door opened, and a gleam of light discovered him to a girl who had looked out on hearing the dogs barking. She thought it was her father arriving from Furnes market; but seeing only a girl, the farmer's daughter accosted her, and asked her business, and the truth was soon told, that she had reached the gates after the *retraite* had been sounded, and that she was looking out for a lodging for the night. She added, however, that which was certainly a slight divergence from truth, that she was going to take service in Furnes.

The farmer's daughter asked her to enter the house, which she did willingly; a few minutes later the farmer arrived, and having heard the story told by Edmund, invited the seeming young female to supper, and told her she should have a lodging for the night. After an hour's talk with the farmer, his wife and daughter, the daughter asked her new female friend whether she would go to bed, saying she should sleep with her. Edmund was rather startled at this proposition, but remembering his costume at once assented.

Arrived in the room, the farmer's daughter began to prepare for bed; but Edmund sat down on a chair and began to reflect on the danger he was in, knowing that the sudden discovery of his sex would very likely lead to loud screams, and certainly then to his arrest. I do not remember the *dénouement*; I only know that Edmund discovered himself to the girl, who promised secrecy and every assistance in her power; and learning from him that he wished to reach the coast, pointed out to him a cross-country footpath, which she assured him would lead him to the seaside, turning the town.

When arrived at the coast, Edmund, who was well provided with money, did not hesitate to knock at the door of a *cabane*, or French fisherman's cottage. The door was opened by a female, and on inquiry it appeared that the husband was off the coast fishing, that he was sure to be home in the evening, as the fishermen dare not go far outward for fear of the English cruisers, and she invited Edmund to wait his return. This he did, but most unfortunately he had resumed his male costume, otherwise he might have laid by for a day or two until Sunday, when almost every fisherman went to mass at Furnes, as he learnt from the fisherman's wife; for he might, had he thought of it in time, have ingratiated himself with the wife, and escaped with the fisherman's boat alone on the Sunday morning, in the same manner he did on a future occasion.

The man returned at dusk, having carried his fish to Furnes; and Edmund, although he had many misgivings, asked him if he could put him on board a cruiser then lying at anchor three or four miles from the shore. The man naturally exaggerated the dangers and difficulties of the attempt, but at length consented to put him on board on payment of one thousand francs. Edmund was very unwilling to part with his money before he was safe on board the frigate; but the man stood firm to his demand, saying that the risk was so great he must go and place the money in the hands of his wife's brother, to be given to his wife in case he should be taken, when he knew that both himself and wife would be searched, and the money taken from them, and that the possession of 40*l.* (1000 *francs*) would be some consolation while in prison. Edmund at length gave way, paid the fisherman the money in French notes, with which he had provided himself at Verdun, and the fisherman took his departure to deposit, as he said, the money with his wife's brother.

Whether the whole statement of the fisherman was a *ruse* to get this money and also the reward for the arrest of an English prisoner, or whether the brother, frightened at the risk to his sister, over-persuaded the fisherman to become traitor, suffice it to say, the man came back from the town, and within a few minutes afterwards a knocking was heard at the door, and the terrible words "*Ouvrez au nom de la loi*" struck the ears of poor Edmund; he was received with scant ceremony by two *gendarmes*, and ordered to march to Furnes and thence to Verdun, keeping his hand on the stirrup of one of them. The annoyance and fatigue of a journey, the greater part on foot, between two French *gendarmes*, and the long distance which separates Furnes from Verdun, was a terrible prospect.

Fortunately a prisoner of war is exempt from search, and Edmund had still some cash in his possession, which he very wisely employed in now and then offering a bottle of "*Longue Bouchon*" to his conductors, and thus got an occasional lift in the saddle when one or other of these gentry was tired of riding; he also got a lift in carts from time to time. At the towns and villages on the road he was sometimes the butt of insolent remarks; sometimes, on the contrary, he became an object of commiseration, particularly among the females.

At length Verdun was reached and he was consigned to a cell in the fortress of Bitche, which was very damp and dark. The following day he was allowed to take a little air in the yard of the prison, when he found that his neighbour in the very next cell was his friend Beamish, who had been arrested about two miles from the frontier, and who complained that his cell was positively two or three inches deep in water. This close imprisonment did not last many days, and the two friends were given better rooms, but their *parole* was refused, under the pretence that they had already committed a breach of *parole*, which was, as my readers know, totally untrue, as they escaped when under arrest, temporary though it might be.

Edmund though much beaten down was not entirely discouraged; he hoped to make his escape and join the English Army, which he knew was in Portugal. Beamish also insisted on casting in his lot with his comrade Edmund.

Their second escape was well contrived: Edmund had plenty of money, and this powerful element he brought into play in bribing a dirty little German Jew, who was in the habit of coming to the prison to buy trinkets or clothes which the prisoners frequently sold to purchase luxuries, which were not included in the prison fare. This little scoundrel screwed a hundred pounds out of Edmund for procuring him the second-hand uniform of a French officer, and the uniform of a French *fantassin*, or infantry soldier, for Beamish. The uniforms once in the prison, they were soon donned, and Edmund marched boldly to the gate, followed by Beamish. The sentry presented arms to the officer, but stopped the linesman Beamish, who wisely held his tongue save only to cry out "*Capitaine!*" on which Edmund turned, and seeing the dilemma, cried out, "*Laissez passer, c'est mon brosseur*"—"Let him pass, it's my brusher," for the French soldiers are not called servants, when employed by the officers, but "Brushers." The two escaped, stepped away at a steady pace until out of sight, when they hurriedly gained the great woods, the paths of which were well known to them when they were still on *parole*.

After some consultation it was determined to take the road towards the south, the distance being very great, and persons proceeding in that direction could scarcely be suspected of being prisoners escaping from Bitche or from Verdun. They once more adopted the plan of travelling at night and lying by in the day. I should mention that by an arrangement with the Jew, they re-exchanged their uniforms for their own clothes in a wood about four miles from their prison, where the Jew met them by appointment. He was to go to a cabaret on the high road, and when he saw the French officer and *fantassin* passing the cabaret, it was agreed he should follow them. He had been given a suit of clothes for each of them when he left them the uniforms, and as he was in the habit of purchasing old clothes, he carried them away without suspicion, and knowing that the two prisoners would leave immediately they could dress themselves, he started direct from the prison for the rendezvous, which by good fortune Edmund and Beamish were enabled to keep. Of course a good deal of chaffing and joking took place on resigning the uniforms and retaking their own dresses and blouses.

The little Jew became very much irritated at some of their observations, for he was asked from whom he had *borrowed* the uniforms, and he feared that the two gentlemen might take him by the throat and force him to disgorge a part of his ill-gotten gains, if they knew he had merely borrowed the dresses, when this searching question was asked in the merest joke, for the joker quite by accident had hit upon the truth; the little Jew was perfectly astounded at their apparent knowledge of the fact of borrowing. After some time spent in frightening the poor devil, he was induced to confess, on the promise that he should keep the money if he told the truth. He then admitted that he had borrowed the uniforms from the wardrobe of a captain who lodged in his house with his *brosseur*, to which last he had given ten *francs* to lie in bed and pretend to be ill, so that he might lend the Jew his uniform for a few hours; therefore the entire 100*l.* went into the little Jew's pocket without requiring him to lay out a single penny beyond the ten *francs*.

The two friends met with no great dangers on their road until they had arrived within ten miles of Angouleme, on the road to Bordeaux, when they were met, just as they were creeping out of a wood, by a *Garde-forestier* or *champêtre*. This worthy individual suspected them of being poachers and insisted on seeing their passports. Here was a dilemma! Beamish had caught the word "passport," and began to fumble in his pocket; the only passport he had was his pass to circulate when on *parole* three leagues or thereabouts round Verdun; Edmund was in the same situation, but seizing Beamish by the arm he whispered to him in English to leave the whole matter to him, Edmund, and to pretend to be unsteady on his legs as if drunk.

Edmund then addressing the *Garde-champêtre,* said to him in French, "Poaching is it you suspect us of? Well, if that is the case we will go home with you, and you can send to the *maire,* and *he* will soon tell you who *we* are."

Of course these words had two meanings; the *Garde* thought his two poachers were friends of *M. le Maire,* Edmund *inwardly* meant the words in quite another sense, as we may easily believe. After walking a few paces very peaceably, Beamish began to stagger and rolled against the *Garde,* who at first thought he was about to be attacked by his prisoners, and seized hold of the hilt of his short sabre; but the next reel of Beamish brought Edmund to the ground, who, rising to his legs, immediately called on the *Garde* for aid, as his friend was so tipsy he could not walk. The *Garde* and Edmund at length got Beamish on his legs, and one on each side, a few paces were got over, when Beamish again pretended to fall on his knees.

Of course, Beamish never opened his mouth, but his friend Edmund began rating him severely in French for making too free with *M. le Comte's* champagne, and asking him what would the countess say if she saw him in this state. The *Garde* with open mouth and ears was taking in the title of count and countess, and at length said, "*Ces Messieurs ont diné avec M. le Comte de la Roche Guyon.*"

Edmund replying in French, asked the *Garde* how he could possibly know this; the *Garde* replied, "Oh, I noticed you gentlemen were coming from the direction of the *château*, but I little thought the gentlemen had been dining with the count."

Edmund, always ready, replied, "Then where the devil do you think we dined?"

The *Garde* now began to think he had got into a scrape in venturing to charge the count's friends with being poachers, and asked what was to be done; as Beamish seemed too drunk to walk, he proposed if he could manage to get him on his shoulders that he would carry him to the *château*, which he said would be hard work, as it was at least a league distant. The news that the *château where they had dined* was between two and three miles distant was very consolatory to Edmund; he began to see his way out of the dilemma. Acceding to the kind offer, he proposed to aid Beamish to mount the shoulders of the stalwart *Garde*. After several attempts, during which Beamish and the *Garde* kissed the sod more than once, the gallant Beamish was mounted and the *Garde* prepared to start for the *château*.

He had scarcely taken three steps when he was suddenly tripped up, Edmund, who was supposed to be supporting Beamish from behind, having placed his leg between those of the *Garde*, who with twelve stone on his withers once more rolled on the ground.

The *Garde* thinking he had tripped up against the root of a tree, begged pardon for his false step, Beamish pretending by his Ah's and Oh's to be much hurt. Edmund asked the *Garde* if there was no place near where his friend could repose until sober, adding, "After all he is not in a state to return to the *château*; and what would the ladies say?"

Once more the *Garde* gave Edmund a hint upon which he lost no time to enlarge. The *Garde* observed, "Oh, for *Mdme. la Comtesse* it's nothing, *ces Messieurs* get tipsy often enough, but *Mdlle. Valerie, sa fille, elle deteste les soulards.*"

"*Mon Dieu*," said Edmund, "is it so? she detests drunkards; we must never let the *pauvre garçon* ruin himself with *Mdlle*."

This last was enough for the *Garde*; for, taking off his cocked hat, to which was attached the tricoloured cockade of the Empire, he bowed respectfully to Edmund, and humbly observed, "That his house was close at hand, and that he would long since have proposed that *les Mes-*

EDMUND AND BEAMISH

sieurs should enter and repose themselves, at all events until (Beamish) *le gentilhomme* was capable of locomotion."

All this time Beamish was reposing on the grass, and Edmund, pretending to be much concerned at his state, stooped down, and whispering in his ear, told him to be quiet and allow himself to be carried. Beamish was once more hoisted on the shoulders of the *Garde*, and took good care to ride quiet. About five minutes' walk brought the party to a snug house situate on the borders of the forest, containing three rooms and what was called the *grenier*, a large room in the roof, in which was a truckle-bed occupied occasionally by any friend who might stay drinking late with the *Garde*, and sometimes by an assistant or two when serious poaching was apprehended.

The *Garde*, who was a married man but without children, on entering said a few words to his wife: Edmund overheard some of the words, "*Amis de Monsieur le Comte.*" In a short time a rabbit was skinned, cut to pieces, and without washing away the blood the pieces were placed in a deep frying-pan with two or three slices of bacon cut into pieces the size of a dice; a piece of butter the size of an egg was thrown into the pan, and two or three onions sliced. All this was put on the wood fire, when the *Garde* left the room and brought in two or three bottles of red *vin du pays*, one of which he uncorked and emptied about one-third of its contents into the pan.

Clean napkins were laid on the table, but no table-cloth, and some slices of very brown bread were cut by the wife and placed on the napkins. In a few minutes the pan was taken from the fire, and the best pieces extracted from it with a fork were placed in the two gentlemen's plates; the gravy or sauce with the bacon and onions was in a manner pushed from the pan with a fork, the pan being canted sufficiently to dispense with the use of a spoon: Edmund told me the dish was excellent. Beamish after many exhortations was prevailed upon to sit upright and pick a little supper, the honest *Garde* telling him there was nothing like eating to set the stomach right. I have given this little detail of the cooking of the rabbit, as I afterwards learnt *this* is the famous dish called *Lapin à la Chasseur*.

After supper the *Garde*, who supped with his wife in the corner of the same principal room or kitchen, proposed to give up his bed to Edmund and his friend. Of course *this* was refused, but it was absolutely necessary before the *Garde* would give up his kind offer, to explain to him that the company of Beamish for the night, drunk as he was supposed to have been, would not be agreeable to Edmund. Beamish was therefore relegated to the truckle-bed in the *grenier*, and Edmund, who had observed that the *Garde's* bedroom had no issue save through the kitchen, was at his request furnished with a mattress, pillow, and blanket, which he contrived to place close to the door of the bedroom, so that the *Garde* could not leave the house without his knowledge.

I omitted to say that Edmund had invented a very complicated story, how his friend Beamish had lost his voice from an accident; that they had come from Bordeaux on a pedestrian expedition, and were returning to that town; that the loss of voice of Beamish was temporary; that he could already pronounce several words, and Beamish was called upon in the morning at breakfast to show his powers of speech by pronouncing words after their very distinct pronunciation by Edmund.

I fear I have lingered too long at the Forest *Garde's* house. At all events the fugitives left very early in the morning; and, as if this terrible *rencontre* was destined to end well, they left the house comfortably seated under the white tilt-cloth of a two-wheeled market-cart, which called at the *Garde's* while they were at breakfast, about five in the morning, to carry to market any little article which the *Garde* had to dispose of. The goods forwarded that morning consisted of two fine buck *chevreuils* (or roe-deer), six or seven hares, and twenty or thirty rabbits, besides the Count de la Roche Guyon's *two friends*, sitting on the back bench behind the driver, his wife, and little son.

The two gentlemen wore blouses of a light grey colour over their clothes, as the custom then was, and which sensible custom has continued until within these few years, if not until the present day, for I saw blouses stripped off on descending from the diligence at Macon, when there on my way to Switzerland four or five years agone. I knew the wearers to be gentlemen of rank. I mention the blouses, as they are useful in concealing difference of rank. As both the gentlemen and the peasant wore blouses, their presence in the cart was not noticed. All went well for two or three hours, when they suddenly stopped at the octroi-gate of Angoulême.

Beamish, who did not understand the words spoken by a gentleman in uniform with a sword by his side, who, putting his foot on the step of the cart or *cariole* and looking under the tilt, said, "*Avez-vous quelque chose à déclarer, Messieurs?*" began to squeeze Edmund's arm, as much as to say, now *you* speak, for I *can't*, and looked greatly relieved when Edmund replied, "*Bien, Monsieur,*" and the military-looking gentleman immediately disappeared.

They now entered the town; it was about eight o'clock a.m., and they drove direct to the market-place. Stopping at the door of a small inn, the game was taken from the cart, and the woman and little boy got out, as it was her business to attend the market, and sell the butter, eggs, cheese, game, &c., which might be entrusted to her and her husband. The driver, now addressing Edmund, told him he was going to a wayside cabaret just outside the town; that his wife remained to settle the octroi dues which had been declared by her to the gentleman in uniform, and sell the goods; that he was going a few miles on the other side of the town after he had baited his horse and refreshed himself, and asked Edmund if he intended to accompany him farther, or preferred to go to an inn in Angoulême.

Edmund and his friend preferred the cabaret, as they knew if any inquiries were made as to who they were, the driver would vouch for their being friends of the *count*. They therefore went to the cabaret and sat down, in the course of an hour, to an excellent *fricandeau* of veal, larded and garnished with spinach, the standing dish on market-days of every cabaret in the kingdom of France.

After the *déjeûner* they once more mounted the *cariole*, when Beamish, who had been very silent, not even continuing the whispered conversation he had hitherto carried on with his friend Edmund, suddenly exclaimed, "My dear Edmund, we *must* separate. I shall certainly cause your arrest and mine too, and I may as well fall alone into the hands of the Philistines."

On Edmund remonstrating, the gallant and kind-hearted Beamish replied, "Nonsense; I cannot always be shamming drunk or pretending to have lost my speech. I have been very near ruining you twice in the last twenty-four hours. You cannot always expect to escape so well as we have done hitherto, and I shall leave you when we arrive at the end of our ride. I shall pretend to be afflicted with stammering if any questions are asked, and with a few rolls and a pound of cheese I can subsist Certainly through the two or three days which my walk to Bordeaux to our rendezvous there will occupy."

Edmund was much perplexed; he knew well enough the danger was much greater in the company of a man who could not speak French save with a most violent Britannic accent, nevertheless he still insisted on not separating, and the gallant Beamish seemed to acquiesce. They arrived at Montmoreau, a small town about fourteen miles farther on the direct road to Bordeaux, and quitted the *cariole* together, after liberally, but not too extravagantly, rewarding the driver, and proceeded together to a cabaret, where they supped and occupied a double-bedded room. Waking early in the morning, Edmund was surprised to find Beamish already up, and his bed deserted. He thought he must be gone down to look after breakfast, and thought further how foolish he was. On descending to the kitchen, the host told him the dumb gentleman left soon after daybreak, leaving a note, which was sealed with a wafer, on the table. The note was short, but expressive:

Goodbye, old friend; we shall meet, I trust, at Bordeaux. I could not continue to peril your chance.

So his gallant friend was gone. We afterwards heard that he was once more taken; but of this I am by no means certain. A few years later, I believe, he fell among the heroes who died on the field of Waterloo. I have no doubt that Edmund's journal would enlighten us on this point, but at all events I have been fortunate in having transcribed a few pages at Lisbon, from whence, and from my own notes and a rather retentive memory, I have drawn these pages.

Edmund once alone ran but little risk; he walked, and sometimes rode, from Montmoreau, where they parted, to Libourne; here he rested a day or two, sending a letter to his countrywoman, Madame Lynch, wife of the then *maire* of Bordeaux. M. Lynch, although born in France, was also of Irish descent. Madame Lynch informed him he might safely approach Bordeaux with the passport she sent him, which was that of a young man of the same age. Once arrived at Bordeaux he was most kindly received by M. and Madame Lynch. The family kept him out of sight when any stranger called; but in a short time a 'passport was procured for him under his own French sounding name, although there was no French blood in his veins, save the drop of pure Norman of the time of the Conqueror.

At all events the passport was very useful—it procured him a pass to amuse himself with a sailing-boat on the Garonne. Of course (as with all passes of the kind) it limited his seaward route to a few hundred of yards before arriving at the station of the Douane, at Test, a little hamlet then, but *now* a fashionable watering-place, at the mouth of the Garonne. This pass or. licence was to be the means of his escape, for he took care to purchase the fastest undecked sailing pleasure-boat he could find, and for weeks took a daily cruise up and down the river, sometimes approaching the limit near the Custom-house station; sometimes, as if by accident, omitting to luff until he was in front of these green-coated gentry.

One day he heard that a French fleet was lying off the coast, about three miles, and a day or two later that the fleet had left and that a small English fleet was lying at anchor on the very same spot. Edmund longed for a gale of wind off the coast and down the last reach of the Garonne. He was at length gratified: having tacked some distance up the stream, with a very light wind, he had not turned to run back ten minutes when it came on to blow hard towards the sea; Edmund thought his hour was come, and running down with all sail set, he was soon opposite the station of the Douane; he had so often overstepped his bounds (or rather oversailed) that the Douaniers paid no attention, when Edmund's black servant, whom he had hired to attend to the boat, began to shout, the cowardly rascal fearing a shot from the Douane.

Edmund, however, soon quieted him, for drawing a pistol from his pocket and pointing it at his head at about three yards' distance, he told him to lie down, and that if he opened his mouth he was a dead man. The servant's voice had, however, reached the ears of the Douane, and Edmund saw four or five men hastily launching a boat about the size of his own. This did not greatly alarm him, for he had a spanking breeze and a good boat, and if nothing gave way, he felt sure he should be under the guns of the English ships before the Douaniers could get within shot of him. He was not disappointed. The Douaniers seeing the flying boat running right under the English guns, thought that discretion was the better part of valour, so emptying their muskets in the direction of Edmund's boat, they gave up the chase, and Edmund had the pleasure of seeing them returning slowly to their post, pulling hard with four oars (their mast taken down) against the breeze which had carried him to safety.

The black man was set free, and ordered to return to Bordeaux, when the wind had dropped the next morning.

Before returning to the narrative of my first march and first bivouac, I may as well mention that circumstances subsequently carried me to Bordeaux when the war was over, although peace had not been proclaimed. I was lodged with my general, Sir John Byng, at the house of the *maire*, M. Lynch; and Madame Lynch told me the story of my cousin Edmund's visit and fortunate escape, (see appendix).

CHAPTER 3

The Battle of Vittoria

I must now return to my personal narrative. I fear I have nothing to tell so amusing as the escapes from Verdun; but at all events I shall give a youngster's impression of war as presented to me.

My first bivouac after the first day's march can never be obliterated from my memory. The novelty, the excitement, the feeling that I was now really a soldier and no longer a "featherbed hero," stirred up my energies. This march took place on the breaking-up of the winter-quarters of the British Army to advance on the French, who were then falling back on Vittoria, to make their final stand in Spain. The pitching the tents when evening came and the day's march was over, the cutting down of trees, the lopping of branches for fires for cooking our rations for our dinner or supper, reminded me of a gigantic picnic; the fine wild scenery around us, and later in the evening the loud buzzing of the insects and the deep-toned croaking of the frogs—all these sounds so much louder than in our more temperate islands—naturally caused a lasting impression; and the novelty of sleeping, or rather attempting to sleep, for the first time under canvas, completely banished sleep from my eyes.

Until the monotonous *tap! tap! tap!* of the drum, seeming to come as it did, from a long distance on the left flank, advancing towards us as its sound was taken up, or rather repeated by regiment after regiment, and passed *us* on to our left flank, warned us that the time of march approached, and that tents must be struck, baggage packed, and ourselves prepared to march, in the course of another half-hour or less. I got off my camp-bed, but the sleepless night and excitement had their effect. I felt heavy and sick, but I soon shook off the temporary indisposition. I am happy to say I never suffered an hour's illness during the war.

Being attached to the Light Infantry Company, I was relieved from baggage guard; so, mounting my pony, I proceeded with the army in the direction of Talavera. After a few days' march we were halted under the walls of that beautiful town, and visited the field where that great and bloody Battle of Talavera had been so lately fought. When arms were piled and the division at rest, I started for the town, and I confess I think I have seen no other town in Spain which can compare with Talavera. Perhaps the open shops and the general feeling of gaiety and security presented in the appearance of the inhabitants, things which we had not yet seen in Spain, may have, induced me to see the town "*en couleur de rose.*"

We were not, however, permitted to linger long at Talavera. The very next morning we heard that our cavalry had had a slight brush with the cavalry of the enemy, who had retreated behind the Tormes, blowing up the bridge behind them. The bridge was quickly repaired, but in a very partial manner, so that we had great difficulty in persuading our horses to cross. However, we got over in safety. I now began to think I smelt powder, and that I was about to experience that curious sensation felt when for the first time bullets are heard whistling about our juvenile ears. I was about to receive what the French have so aptly named "*Le baptême de feu.*"

We marched rapidly across a most verdant and luxuriant country. We left Valladolid in view on our right, many of us very much desiring to see the inside, as well as the outside of its walls, but we were disappointed. We neither saw Valladolid nor Madrid.

Every morning, for we were now in June, the *tap! tap! tap!* of the now familiar drum awoke us to face a burning sun; for, however early we started, we were nearly roasted alive before nine o'clock. But we forgot all our fatigue and marched briskly on our way with the earnest desire of overtaking the retreating French Army. We were, however, halted for three days at Urbado, from whence the now to us familiar name of Urbado Camp. On the third day we continued our march; the troops were in splendid condition, both as regards health and discipline, and we well knew that a great battle was imminent; which proved to be a well-founded belief, for our march eventually terminated at Vittoria, where that great and glorious battle was fought which put an end to the French power in Spain. I shall now take the liberty of saying a few words respecting our enemies the French.

There seemed to be a national antipathy between the French and the Spaniards, and as pleasant and gentlemanly a feeling between the

English and the French. I may mention, as an example of this feeling, a circumstance which occurred, I may almost say to myself, at all events within my immediate knowledge. I was sent three or four miles to the front, with a picquet of thirty men. We occupied a sort of farmhouse, called a "*quinta*," about a mile from the French lines: it was near Roncesvalles, on the road to St. Jean Pied du Port. It was well known to the French that we were at the *quinta*, for the scouts came close to us several times, but we were there three days unmolested.

They knew from their scouts also when we were relieved by a party of General Morillo's Spanish soldiers. The same night they relieved us, they were attacked and all taken prisoners. It was evident enough they did not want us. We frequently found a French soldier, and sometimes a French officer, at a spring, a quarter of a mile in our front—I mean in front of the *quinta*. There was always an exchange of civilities between the Red and Blue, but I well know that a Spaniard would have been fired on without remorse, and *vice versâ*. The Spaniards were excusable in *their* hate, as the French were *invaders*, but why the French hated the Spaniards so violently I never knew; but probably the guerilla fighting in the earlier part of the war, which was a most bloody species of warfare, may have been the cause.

At all times when we were in a country which looked like sporting, we got out our shotguns, for I must, as we are talking of campaigning, explain that we did not get out our rifles or old Brown Besses, and being, as I have just said, on a gentlemanly footing with the enemy, we made many sporting excursions with more or less success. The most remarkable one I recollect, both from the extraordinary quantity and quality of the game met with and the empty bags which went home, induces me to mention it. While at the Urbado Camp, which lies in a fine, flat agricultural-looking plain of many miles in extent, we heard that the plain abounded with game, particularly with bustards. A party was therefore formed to circumvent these splendid birds. A number of soldiers offered their services as beaters, and a keen sportsman, Captain Blomer, Colonels Leith, Nicolls, and Knox, with the young subaltern, myself, formed the party.

We were soon equipped, and under the orders of Captain Blomer we proceeded towards that part of the plain on which the bustards had been seen. It was, as I have before observed, the month of June, not a very sporting season of the year; but as the hen bustards were sitting closely, it was not likely we should fall in with more than one or two, perhaps by stumbling over their nests. But the cock bustard was our quarry, these fine birds being in the habit of assembling on an open space on the plain, and strutting about with their wings scraping the ground like a village-gobbler, as they say in America, or turkey-cock.

It was not long before the keen eye of Blomer detected the birds going through their morning performance of strutting and blowing. We were immediately halted, and told to take up positions in line behind bushes, stones, or hillocks, to remain perfectly quiet, and wait for the birds. Blomer, with his beaters, took a long detour, and throwing his right and left wings forward, he advanced slowly on the birds, with the view of driving them to pass over our heads. I could hear my own heart beat so loud that I was almost afraid the birds would hear it.

Suddenly we saw the whole flock rise; a shot was fired behind them, and they all came down upon us. Some flew right over my head, and over the heads of my brother sportsmen; some flew to the right or left of us; they certainly were long shots, but after a general discharge not a bird fell. Without boasting of myself I may say we were all good game shots; but whether it was the excitement caused by the novelty and size of the game, or whether it was the poor quality of our ammunition, of which I spoke before, not a feather did I see fall. We had spent a long morning in the attempt to make a bag. We had outmanoeuvred the feathered enemy, but we returned hungry to camp without a trophy of war either in the shape of killed, wounded, or prisoners. We only brought home empty bags and most formidable appetites.

Once more I must return to our march, for I left our troops some miles in advance. We had now got into a hilly country. A spur from the mountains ran down to the river. The high road—a good and wide one—ran between the spur of the hill and the river. Morillo and his fine Spanish division, attached to Lord Hill's corps, were now close up with us. We followed the road, and suddenly turning the hip or spur of the hill or mountain, we saw before us the great plain of Vittoria, with the whole French army in position. I will now give my impressions of a great battle.

The Battle of Vittoria.

I do not pretend, as a subaltern, to give a strategic account of this great battle. I shall confine myself to an outline of the scene, the movement, the smoke, the din, and the carnage. I shall endeavour to describe my own feelings and doings in this my first engagement. As, however, these events happened more than half a century since, I may remind my readers that our army on the field of Vittoria was commanded in chief by Lord Wellesley, the *corps d'armée* in which I was a subaltern by Sir Rowland Hill. The Spaniards under Morillo were attached to our corps, and the Portuguese were under General Buchan. The troops were confident in their generals, and of victory. My corps stood to its arms on arriving on the field; the tents and baggage were sent to the rear; the dismounted officers were informed that they must quit the saddle, and my capital little English pony was handed over to Antonio, my Portuguese boy, with orders to join the baggage-guard with the other horses.

It was about eight o'clock in the morning; the sun was now well above the horizon, and assumed the shape of a huge crimson ball; it was the early sun of the 21st of June, the longest day in the year, now about to be the witness of a great, glorious, though bloody battle. The French Army, although they had been retreating, were encumbered with plunder, which they were endeavouring to carry off into France; but we saved them further trouble on this score. The sight of this great army of enemies made a deep impression on the mind of so young a soldier. The town of Vittoria, about three miles to our left, was indistinctly visible. The left of the French army rested on the heights abutting on the River Zadora, and was thrown forward very considerably in advance of the town; but we could easily trace the French line until it seemed to entangle itself in an enormous mass of all sorts of guns, waggons, tumbrels, &c., &c., which covered a large portion of the plain.

The moment was a most exciting one. As we marched up to our post in line of battle, I observed a man lying on his back a little to my left. I could not resist going over to look at the body; it was that of a young Frenchman who had evidently died that morning—but from what cause I did not ascertain. It was the first dead body I had seen on the field, and caused a painful and sickening sensation, which, however, was shortly to be passed by, as death on the field became a matter of common occurrence.

We shortly after this arrived at the base of a slightly elevated piece of ground, where we halted, our general wishing to place us in as safe a position as he could, while the rear of the army was coming up, and forming in line of battle. A cannon-ball from the French lines speedily informed us that we were not quite protected, and also that the French had exactly discovered our distance; and the ball passed through our column, scattering the brains of one or two of our soldiers upon their comrades. This began to look like business. We were, however, ordered to pile arms, a few of the light company retaining theirs, and forming in front to keep up the appearance of skirmishing with the French sharpshooters, who occupied a wood in considerable numbers exactly in our front, and between the lines of the two armies. A sharp firing on the right gave us notice that the ball had been opened in that quarter. It was Morillo's Spanish division that had come in contact with the most advanced part of the French Army.

The Spaniards, though acting admirably under their patriotic and gallant general, were unable to make much impression on the French troops, until they were reinforced by a British battalion sent to their assistance. This was that brave regiment the 71st Highlanders, under the command of one of the best and most experienced officers in the army, Colonel Cadogan. Soon a rumour passed through our column, as we lay in our position, that he had fallen, which was very quickly confirmed by an *aide-de-camp*, who arrived to our general, and the news was received with deep emotion by our officers, most of whom knew and admired him. We had, however, short time for lamentation.

The rear of the army had already arrived in their position, and the order "Stand to your arms!" was given, and very quickly responded to. Our light companies, of which mine was one, were ordered to form in extended skirmishing order, in front of the brigade, and were directed to advance and clear the wood, from which the sharpshooters were annoying us, and at whom I had myself taken several shots from the musket of the corporal of my company. A field of corn, standing four or five feet high, and just ready for the sickle, was between us and the wood, and as we advanced through it, besides the bullets from the wood, an occasional cannonball bowled along through it, its course being easily seen by the lowering of the ears of corn, as if reaped. As they rolled through it, I felt as if I could have stopped some of these balls with my foot, they appeared to roll so slowly. Fortunately for me I did not try the experiment, as the loss of a leg would have ensued.

As we approached the wood, the fire from it slackened, and we entered and passed through without meeting much opposition; but when we emerged at the opposite side, we saw the dark line of the French army, still in their position, within point-blank distance. A perfect hailstorm of bullets was poured down upon us, which, if it had lasted, must have swept us all into eternity. But we pushed forward, and the French turned. Looking to my right, I saw my captain, Girdlestone, wounded and supported by the bugler. I rushed over to him;

he seized me by the hand, gave it a hard squeeze, and said to me, "Go on, my boy! your name will be mentioned."

I felt a certain choking sensation in my throat; a tear swelled into my eye, but it had not time to fall. I ran on frantically to the front, screaming at the top of my voice, "Come on, 31st!" which cry could not have reached the ears of the half of my company, in consequence of the roar of the battle. But these brave fellows did not require to be called to advance; the only difficulty was to keep them back.

The bugler, whose name was Butterworth, whom I had left supporting Girdlestone, had again joined, and continued to sound the advance, which he never for a moment omitted to do from the time the word was given. I was parched with thirst from the heat and excitement, when an officer attached to the light company of the Buffs, seeing me panting for breath, dipped his hand, on which was a thick glove, into a ditch, which was more blood than water, and passed it across my mouth, which greatly refreshed me. By the wound of Girdlestone I found myself placed in command of the light company of the 31st, who had been through the greater part of the Peninsular War, and, though reduced in numbers, were as gallant a lot of men as ever existed.

I began to feel that, at the age of sixteen, I was placed in a very responsible position, and determined to keep myself as cool and steady as was possible. I had hardly time to make this determination when I heard a tremendous rush on our left; the ground seemed actually to quake under me, and, looking in the direction of the sound, I saw the whole British host—artillery, cavalry, and infantry—throwing themselves on the line of the French Army. Three or four regiments of cavalry were at the moment charging, and galloped up to the foot of the eminence on which the French line stood; it was too steep for the horses to ascend, and they were obliged to wheel. But the firm and uncompromising style in which the British Army advanced was too much for the nerves of the French; they turned in retreat along their whole line, and the Battle of Vittoria was won.

For the rest of the day it was easy work for us. In looking towards the town of Vittoria, I saw a moving mass of all sorts of vehicles retiring over the plain; it was the whole of the *matériel* of the French army, their baggage and their plunder. Notwithstanding their hasty retreat, the whole fell into the hands of Lord Wellington's army. Here was taken the famous Berlin, fitted up with every convenience and luxury, with silver and Sèvres china: this was the travelling-carriage of King

Joseph, and which in after-years delighted the eyes of our children at Madame Tussaud's. The battle had raged to a much more intense degree far away to our left, in the neighbourhood of the town of Vittoria, and in some instances swept right through it; but, as I did not see it, I will not pretend to describe it. It has now become a matter of history, from Lord Wellington's despatches and other competent authorities.

Indeed, we were ignorant of almost every detail of the action, save those which passed under our own observation, until we received the English newspapers some time afterwards; but it is well known how complete was the defeat: 150 guns, the whole of Joseph Buonaparte's personal baggage, and, as I before observed, his carriage, fell into the hands of our army. I regret to say, but am scarcely surprised at it, that there were some breaches of discipline,—now known under the Indian name of "looting,"—which were severely censured, and in some instances punished; but it would be invidious to name any particular regiment after all had otherwise behaved so well.

The French are first-rate hands at running away when once they are panic struck; and although we passed rapidly over the plain in pursuit, we could not again come up to them. While thus in pursuit, I observed a large body of men moving parallel with us on our right. I said to an officer near me, "Those fellows are French."

He said, "No, they are Spaniards."

I, however, was right, and if we could have informed one of the commanders of our cavalry, they would every one of them have been taken prisoners. A couple of squadrons would have been enough. Seeing us, they rapidly moved off. The ground, as we marched forward, was strewed with all sorts of papers, letters, &c., and, as I passed along, I occasionally picked up a loose paper. Sometimes it was a love-letter, and sometimes a touching effusion from a beloved mother or sister to some young French soldier. The firing had nearly ceased, but an occasional flying shot from a gun enlivened us.

Almost the last shot that was fired—for it was now near evening—I heard whistling along exactly in my direction. The usual feeling is to dip the head, and thus make a low bow to these dangerous missiles, as they generally fly over head. This ball was, however, flying low, and, as it rushed up to me, an involuntary impulse caused me to jump as high as I could; and, at the moment, I thought it was a fortunate jump for me, as the cannon-ball seemed to strike exactly on the spot I had been standing upon, and passed to the rear, leaving me uninjured.

We continued the pursuit of the French until dark, when we were halted, and had to make ourselves as comfortable as we could, without our baggage or tents. A double allowance of rum, was, however, served out, and a small piece of raw beef, cut from some bullocks which had been driven in, hastily killed and cut up, and almost as quickly grilled at the point of the bayonet or ramrod. As soon as the toasted beef was swallowed, we lay down upon the bare ground, which fortunately was quite dry; and my gallant Colonel, Leith, Captains Nicholls and Knox, and myself slept under one blanket. I happened to get a centre berth under the aforesaid blanket, in which there was a long split, which just came to my share. I was too much fatigued to take notice why I felt so chilled, but I slept like a top until the assembly was sounded before daybreak the next morning, when I found I had been sleeping with the window (query blanket?) open.

Before daybreak we were standing to our arms; the old three taps of the morning drum did not now come into play. We again started in pursuit of the French in the direction of Roncesvalles, famous for its battle mentioned in the *Song of Roland*, where "Roland the Brave and Oliver, and every paladin and peer on Roncesvalles fell." We had not gone far before we found an abandoned gun, making up the tale of 151. I really believe this was the villainous tube which threw the shot so near me and made me jump for my life. In a short time we came to Pampeluna. The French threw a garrison into this strongly-fortified town, but had not time to provision it; they had provisions only for a very short time.

We passed by without any apprehension of leaving so strong a place in our rear, as it was to be surrounded and blockaded by the Spaniards, who were already in force on the spot. The rear of retreating and defeated army leaves many a record of its passage, in dead and dying men, and horses more or less severely wounded, and various sorts of debris such as broken waggons, and useless arms, knapsacks, etc., etc. We took little notice or care for these objects, and left even valuable muskets on the road as we passed. After a few hours we reached the town of Roncesvalles, which is at the foot of the Pyrenees, where we halted.

The town was not imposing; a few small houses, a couple of rather large monastical-looking buildings, which we soon ascertained had been converted into Posadas. We were not long in seeking the interior of the buildings to ascertain what good things we could procure to appease our ravenous appetites. The viands produced were cooked with the usual quantity of garlic, so grateful to the Spanish appetite, but so uncongenial to the English stomach; but hunger is an admirable sauce, and we really enjoyed our repast.

Late in the evening our baggage, &c., came up, our tents were soon pitched, and those who had not ensconced themselves in the few houses were again comfortably in bivouac in their tents. I forgot to mention that my Portuguese boy, Antonio, had the talent to find me out during the night, when I was sleeping under the torn blanket; he brought me my pony, cloak, and blanket. This boy was frequently the butt of the soldier's jokes, which he took very patiently. Among others, when rations of meat were served out in the usual manner by a kind of lottery, performed by placing a soldier with his back to the table or ground, where the rations were laid out, another soldier, pointing to a piece of meat, would call out, "This," meaning, "Who is this for?" when the soldier with his back to the table would name a comrade at hazard, as the recipient of the piece of meat. Sometimes he would call out "*Ista*," pointing to a bad, bony morsel, and the response was inevitably Antonio, or Portugee boy; for, by using the word "*ista*" the Spanish for "this," it was intended to inform the soldier that it was a bad piece, *good for the Portuguese boys*.

The next day our light companies were informed that they would be required to make a sort of secret movement, in as light marching order as possible. This was to a place about three miles to the front, on the road to St. Jean Pied de Port. Our *commandant*, I believe, had sealed orders, not to be opened till after our arrival at the *quinta*, which I before mentioned when speaking of the feelings of the French towards us, and towards the Spaniards.

The country was in all the gorgeous beauty of midsummer, the trees many of them fruit-bearing: cherry-trees were plentiful, with quantities of fruit—ripe and delicious they were in the sultry heat. Things altogether seemed very much altered for the better; we had, in fact, passed the frontier into France, which had not been ravaged by war like unhappy Spain and Portugal, and we were the first of the "enemies' troops," over the French frontier.

We had thus the satisfaction of being the first to enter the territory of *La Belle France* and the Grande Empire. We took up our quarters for the night in and about the *quinta*; but kept a sharp look out, as we were on rather dangerous ground. The rear-guard of the French Army was, as before said, halted in a small village a mile or two in our front, and the sealed orders were that early in the morning we were to make a dash at the village, rush through it without firing a shot, and make prisoners of this small rear-guard if possible.

We should probably have succeeded had it not been for a German soldier of the single company of the 60th Rifles attached to our little light brigade. He could not resist the opportunity of firing a shot into the village before we had reached it. The report, of course, alarmed the little garrison, who were instantly on the move, and, with the rapidity of French soldiers, the greater part of them escaped. "When we returned to Roncesvalles, a Spanish picquet occupied the *quinta*, and that night the Spaniards in return were surprised by the French, and every one of them made prisoners, as I have related previously."

CHAPTER 4

In the Pyrenees

On our return from the *quinta*, in front of Roncesvalles, on the lower road to St. Jean Pied de Port, we encamped again for a few days. My gun, as usual, was soon in requisition, to ascertain if any game was to be found in the neighbourhood. We found that quails were rather numerous, but having no dogs to point or rouse them, we found it very difficult to get them on the wing, the birds being very young, and lying like-stones. Our attention was soon turned from these agreeable pastimes, as an order came for the light companies to move to the front. We were shortly on the move again, and were led up a very narrow road leading us to the top of the Pyrenees, scarcely wide enough to admit the wheels of a 6-pounder. As we marched up this mountainside, I observed for the first time the curious effect of the cloud or mist *pouring* over the brow of the mountain, or through the defiles, which I expected every moment to come down in a heavy shower; but it turned out that it was only the mist.

After a march of about three miles we arrived at the summit of the Pyrenees, and saw the fertile valleys of France spread out before us as if on a map. Here finding a plateau of natural growth, we were ordered to pitch our tents, and make ourselves as comfortable as we could, which we were certainly well inclined to do. I slept like a top, after the fatigues of the day, and began the next morning to look about me and admire the magnificent scenery that lay before, around, and almost at our feet; the fine woods of well-grown trees furnished the sides of the mountains more than halfway up to our elevated position or bank. The rendezvous or alarm-post was pointed out to us, which we were ordered to repair to in case of any movement of the enemy in our front, and every precaution taken to prevent a surprise, by sending outlying pickets, &c.

We soon began to find ourselves tolerably comfortable. The eagle and the vulture, sure accompaniments of an army in the field, which provides ample provender for them, soared over our heads in splendid circles of flight, and I soon began to think of my gun, and what chance there was of sport. I sallied out by myself to prospect the country; looking down from those sublime heights upon the valleys below were the noble woods that adorned the sides of the mountain. I saw little chance of finding any game in these high and wild regions, except perhaps the chance of coming on a bear, if I ventured into the woods, as I heard that they were to be found in these regions.

After amusing myself for half an hour in starting a large stone to roll down the mountain side, until it came with a crash into the forest of trees, some half-mile or so below, quite forgetting where it might eventually go to, or on whose head at the bottom it might possibly fall, I lay down on the side of the mountain to rest myself a little. I was surprised to see just at my elbow a delicious-looking ripe strawberry, and then another and another, and found that the ground was covered with them. After regaling myself on this delicious god-send, I lost very little time in returning to camp, and reporting to my brother officers the treasure I had hit upon, when there was an instantaneous rush to the strawberry-beds, such as I should suppose might in these days happen in the rush to the gold-diggings.

The time hung heavily enough on our hands in this elevated camp for several days; I could not even turn my gun to any account, except an occasional shot, at a long distance, at an eagle or a vulture as he circled over our heads. Sometimes these disgusting birds, when heavily gorged with their prey, would allow us to approach within a few yards, when they with difficulty arose from the ground or rock on which they were seated, but I never, unfortunately, was prepared for such a chance. It is true, however, that we were frequently interested by the reports that we heard of what was going on in our front.

When the news reached the emperor that the Ebro had been passed, the Battle of Vittoria won, and the French Army beaten and disorganised, driven into France, and the French territory violated by the feet of the enemy, Bonaparte, who was then in the north, and whose luck had begun to turn, despatched Marshal Soult in hot haste to reorganize the French Army, and endeavour to recover the lost ground.

The marshal, who was supposed to be the best general under his command, lost no time in obeying his orders. He collected every man that he could lay his hands on, and sent them to the Spanish frontier by every conceivable means he could procure. Waggons, coaches, and every means of conveyance were pressed into the service, and in an incredibly short period he had assembled a force, as he thought, sufficient to drive the redcoats backward to the Ebro and into the sea. Rumours reached us daily of what was preparing for us, and on the 23rd of July he issued his famous manifesto to his army; and as it has probably never reached the ears of many of the present generation I do not hesitate to give it here, though it has often, I conclude, been published and perused with interest by many who must have passed away. It was dated from St. Jean Pied de Port, and is as follows:—

Proclamation of Marshal Soult.
(To be read at the heads of companies in each regiment, 23rd July, 1813.)

Soldiers! The recent events of the war have induced His Majesty the Emperor to invest me, by an Imperial decree of the 1st instant, with the command of the armies of Spain, and to honour me with the flattering title of his 'Lieutenant.' This high distinction cannot but convey to my mind sensations of gratitude and joy, but they are not unalloyed with regret at the train of events which have, in the opinion of His Majesty, rendered such an appointment necessary in Spain.

It is known to you, soldiers, that the enmity of Russia, roused into active hostility by the eternal enemy of the Continent, made it incumbent that numerous armies should be assembled in Germany early in the spring. For this purpose were many of your comrades withdrawn. The emperor himself assumed the command, and the arms of France, guided by his powerful and commanding genius, achieved a succession of as brilliant victories as any that adorn the annals of our country. The presumptuous hopes of aggrandisement entertained by the enemy were confounded, pacific overtures were made, and the emperor, always inclined to consult the welfare of his subjects by following moderate counsels, listened to the proposals that were made.

While Germany was thus the theatre of great events, that enemy, who, under pretence of succouring the inhabitants of the Peninsula, has in reality devoted them to ruin, was not inactive. He assembled the whole of his disposable force, English, Spaniards, and Portuguese, under his most experienced officers, and, relying upon the superiority of his numbers, advanced in three divisions against the French force assembled upon the Douro.

With well-provided fortresses in his front and rear, a skilful general, enjoying the confidence of his troops, might, by selecting good positions, have braved and discomfited his motley levy. But unhappily at this critical period timorous and pusillanimous counsels were followed. The fortresses were abandoned and blown up, hasty and disorderly marches gave confidence to the enemy, and a veteran army, small indeed in number, but great in all that constitutes the military character, which had fought, bled, and triumphed in every province in Spain, beheld with indignation its laurels tarnished and itself compelled to abandon all its acquisitions—the trophies of many a well-fought and bloody day.

When, at length, the indignant voice of the troops arrested this disgraceful flight, and its commander, touched with shame, yielded to the general desire, and determined upon giving battle near Vittoria, who can doubt from this generous enthusiasm, this fine sense of honour, what would have been the result had the general been worthy of his troops; had he, in short, made those dispositions and movements which would have secured to one part of his army the co-operation and support of the other?

Let us not, however, defraud the enemy of the praise which is due to him; the dispositions and arrangements of their general have been prompt, skilful, and consecutive. The valour and steadiness of his troops have been praiseworthy. Yet do not forget that it is to the benefit of your example they owe their present military character, and that whenever the relative duties of a French general and his troops have been ably fulfilled, their enemies have commonly had no other resource than flight. Soldiers, I partake of your chagrin, your grief, your indignation; I know that the blame of the present situation of the army is imputable to others; be the merit of repairing it yours. I have borne testimony to the emperor of your bravery and zeal.

His instructions are to drive the enemy from those lofty heights, which enable them proudly to survey our fertile valleys, and chase them across the Ebro. It is on the Spanish soil that your tents must next be pitched, and from thence your resources drawn. No difficulties can be insurmountable to your valour and devotion.

Let us, then, exert ourselves with mutual ardour, and be assured that nothing can give greater felicity to the paternal heart of the emperor than the knowledge of the triumphs of his army, of its increasing glory, of its having rendered itself worthy of him and of our dear country.

Extensive but combined movements for the relief of the fortresses are upon the eve of taking place. They will be completed in a few days. Let the account of our success be dated from Vittoria, and the birth of his Imperial Majesty be celebrated in that city, so shall we render memorable an epoch deservedly dear to all Frenchmen.

Soult, Duc de Dalmatie,
Lieutenant de l'Empereur.

I may as well remark that the blockade of Pampeluna was still manfully maintained by the Spaniards, and the siege of St. Sebastian, after some fruitless attempts to storm it, by which our army sustained great loss, was still continued. We could hear the roar of the cannon almost continuously, though we were at a considerable distance, ours being the extreme right of the British lines. There was only one pass a few miles to our right, called the Pass of Jaca, or Haca as pronounced, which was occupied by the Spaniards. The other two British Brigades of our division, that is, the Highland Brigade and O'Callaghan's Brigade, occupied the pass of Maya, several miles to our left; and Sir Lowry Cole's division also occupied some intermediate position.

On the evening of the 24th we were apprised that something might be expected, and desired to be particularly on the alert. We had been in the habit of standing to our arms an hour before daybreak, and not returning to our camp until we could see a grey horse a mile off. On the morning of the 25th, however, as soon as we could distinguish anything at the front, we saw that the French were coming up, and forming themselves in columns to our front, and we began to see that we were about to have another brush with the enemy, and that they were going to try the experiment under the distinguished and powerful commander, Marshal Soult. They continued to bring up their columns for several hours; I conclude that the miserable state of the roads did not admit of any very rapid movements.

A spur of the mountain ran down for a short space to our left. Our position was a rocky eminence, entirely composed of large rocks, an admirable position for light troops to occupy. The road to the front passed just on the right of this eminence, and there shortly after our arrival I saw General Morillo, mounted on a tall black Spanish horse, with long white military gloves which came nearly to his elbow, and which he kept continually pulling up, as it appeared to me by a sort of nervous movement. He sent out a lot of his Spaniards to skirmish in the front; and we were ordered to defend our position to the last extremity, a duty which we performed with the usual pluck and determination of British soldiers.

At length, about one or two o'clock, we observed the whole of the French Army in our front advancing to the attack. The Spanish skirmishers were of course soon driven in, and a cloud of French sharpshooters were thrown in thousands against us. With great gallantry, and before very long, they arrived at the foot of the rocky eminence that we were left to defend to the last, of course to give time to our general to retire his brigade, which it was evident was the inevitable result of the attack of so large a force on one brigade. We kept the rocky position, as we were ordered, to the last, and it was not until the French sharpshooters were mingling with our men that we saw the necessity of retreating; our left was also turned by the French troops. We had a considerable space to traverse before we could be safe from the fire, behind a spur of the hill in our rear, and we had to make for it. I confess I was greatly inclined to have a run for it, but I recollected what an example it would be to our men, and besides I had a great repugnance to *running* away.

However, I walked as speedily as I could, particularly as the French bullets were constantly striking the side of the hill all about me, and it was with much satisfaction I at last found myself under a certain degree of protection, with most of my men in pretty good condition, and few killed or wounded. The French seemed satisfied with having driven us from our position, and inclined to follow us up slowly. The general had retired the brigade in the direction of Roncesvalles, and as we got a little to the rear he halted the light companies, and, with tears in his eyes, thanked them for the gallant stand they had made in their position.

We did not remain long to rest ourselves, but followed the brigade down the hill in the direction of Roncesvalles. As we descended the hill I was walking alongside of the general on horseback, and feeling the gravel rather penetrating my foot, I turned it up to Sir John, and showed him the bare skin of my foot, both shoe and stocking being worn through. He said, "There is one of my mules that is not gone to the rear with the baggage, and I think I have a pair of shoes that I will lend you," which he did when we got down to the town, but remarked at the same time, "I shall not be ashamed to take them back when we next see our baggage," which I promised faithfully and performed, though they were nearly by that time in the state of my old cast-off ones.

We passed Roncesvalles, pursuing our retreat in the direction of Pampeluna, and marched on rather dejected until night began to gather in about us, when at length we were ordered to halt, light our fires, and commence our cooking, the tents and baggage still far to the rear. We had not accomplished this interesting performance when the bugle sounded to fall in, and we were ordered to put out our fires. In fact, the French were close on our track. I now began to discover the difference between a victorious advance and a retreat in face of the enemy. We trudged along all night in the dark.

I was so sleepy that I could not keep my eyes open, and once or twice lay down to endeavour to get a little rest; but the feet of the retreating soldiers soon roused me from my precarious rest, and on standing up at one particular place, I observed a gentleman in a blue military frock-coat and a round hat, riding in the opposite direction to that we were going, and I heard him say, "Right about, right about. It is —— odd if 10,000 British cannot show their faces to 30,000 Frenchmen." It was Picton; his division was in the rear, and we were falling back upon it: however, his gleam of hope did not last long, and we were soon on the line of retreat again.

As the day dawned upon us we were in sight of Pampeluna, some distance on our left, encompassed with clouds of Spanish cavalry and infantry blockading the town, and as we passed over the summit of a rather high hill or mountain we saw the French Army making a most determined attack on the British. We commanded the view, which was magnificent; and the first thing that met my eye was a battalion of Portuguese scattered and running like mad, and immediately a large body of French formed themselves *en masse* on our position. I thought things were beginning to look bad, but immediately afterwards I saw a regiment of redcoats go at the French column like bull-dogs.

I must say the French stood their ground wonderfully, and for a moment or two it appeared to me doubtful what the issue would be; but just as this gallant regiment got within a few paces of the French column, I saw the two colours go out in front of our heroes almost up to the French bayonets, the battalions following them true as steel, when they hurled the Frenchmen down the steep face of the Pyrenean mountain that they expected to drive us from. This regiment was the 21st Fusiliers. I asked afterwards who the gallant youths were who carried the colours with such commendable effect, and was informed that one of them was Francis Russell, in whose room I and the second Marquis of Anglesey slept at Westminster; and we were both his fags. "Hoorah for Westminster!" said I.

Our battalion immediately moved down to the spot on which I saw this brilliant charge executed: there was a little square plot, about the size of an Irishman's potato-garden, surrounded by a low wall about one foot and a half high, within this space lay eight dead bodies—six French, one Portuguese, and the other English. An unfortunate French sergeant, shot through the lungs, and evidently in mortal agony, made such a row, that my general asked me to see him moved to a small house in the rear. Though the action was, I may say, concluded, I felt as if it was turning my back on the enemy: I, however, obeyed my general's orders, had him carried to the house, where I found the surgeon at work, got him a glass of water, for which he returned me thanks, with a squeeze of my hand, and I returned as quickly as possible to my company.

We halted exactly on the spot where I had seen the fine charge of the fusiliers executed a few minutes before; the dead bodies lay before us, and we remained, until the evening set in, exactly in the same position, looking at the French army on the face of the mountain exactly opposite to us. They did not show any intention of renewing the attack upon us, but, on the contrary, as the day closed in, the French soldiers and our own men got the water from the same small stream that flowed in the valley between us, and we met on the most friendly footing for that purpose. We could distinctly hear the bands of, the different French regiments play, and so near, that we could distinguish the air.

I recollect one in particular, that we afterwards discovered from two bandsmen who had deserted, and came over to us, and were immediately taken into our band, to whom they taught it. It was called Bonaparte's March, and a very fine piece of music it was; I remember the air of it to the present day. When night set in, I lay down in my camlet cloak which Antonio, my Portuguese boy, had brought up to me towards evening, and slept like a top until wakened up by some mounted officer riding at full speed over me. I felt the horse's legs as they caught in my cloak, but the horse, as I believe is usually the case, avoided trampling upon me. It was probably some *aide-de-camp* despatched with a message to some other of our generals, or perhaps to the Spaniards around Pampeluna, for he was going in that direction, but I never discovered who he was.

My own gallant captain, Girdlestone, having recovered from his wound at Vittoria (it was merely a flesh wound through the thigh), had rejoined us this morning; he came up, looking as well and as fresh as paint, which we all rejoiced to see, but he had a bright new regimental coat on, and very clean white trousers, which I suppose made him a conspicuous mark to the French sharpshooters, for before the day was over he was again wounded exactly in the same place, and he had again to return to be nursed through his second wound at Vittoria. I scarcely had time to speak to him, so short was the interval before he was again wounded.

The next morning we, as usual, stood to our arms before daylight, not knowing what important events were before us during the day. There was a good deal of anxiety about where the sixth division was, which report said was moving in our direction; the enemy did not show any symptoms of wishing to renew the battle, in fact they seemed to have had enough of it, and we remained the greater part of the day looking at each other. Towards evening, however, we heard that the sixth division was approaching, and with it "Wellington himself." The moment we heard this every man in the British Army knew and felt that all was right, and we waited perfectly patient for the next move.

Nothing further took place with us that evening; we remained exactly in the same position, and when we had sufficient light the next morning to see what was before us, we observed that the French army was retiring; in fact, Wellington had turned their position and saved us the trouble of going at them in front. Before many hours were over one of the finest spectacles of the campaign occurred; the French army, retreating, had thrown out a cloud of skirmishers to cover it; our army was immediately in motion to follow them up. Our brigade formed the head of the column, and our light companies were thrown out in front to reply to the French sharpshooters. The scenery was magnificent, the day bright and sunshiny. Between our extended line of skirmishers, which extended across the valley, and the head of the column rode Lord Wellington and a splendidly-mounted staff.

It was exactly like a brilliant field-day, or sham fight, although occasionally a bullet passed from front to rear, or *vice versâ*. In this form we advanced during the greater part of the day, until the French began to think it was nearly time to halt for the night and bivouac; and to give us notice of this their intention, they increased the number of their sharpshooters, and treated us to a very sharp fire for some little time. At length we took the hint, and gave up any further attack upon them that evening, as all they seemed to want was time to get away.

The next morning we were very early on the alert, driving the French army before us through the magnificent valley of the Bastan. Towards the middle of the day our general got information that the provisions destined for the relief of Pampeluna were halted in the beautiful secluded village of Elizondo, about a couple or three miles in our front. He determined to make a dash at them; our light companies were delighted at the prospect when they were desired to leave their knapsacks, and anything that would impede their rapid progress, behind for the battalion to carry after them, and away we went at the double. We soon arrived at Elizondo, took the whole convoy, and were told that the French general as he evacuated the town with his troops, was heard to say, "*Doucement, mes enfans.*"

He could not, however, persuade them to wait for us, and we found ourselves in possession of a number of casks of brandy, bread, biscuits, and other creature comforts. The general, fearing the soldiers would get at the brandy, had the casks stove in, and let the brandy run about the street, and it was a sight to see the soldiers lying down on their faces and lapping it up with their hands. We suffered no loss in this charming little episode, except one, alas! a serious one to me. When we set off at the double, I gave my pony to Antonio, wishing to go on foot with my men. We left the brigade a considerable way in the rear. A small detachment of French cavalry by some accident got between us and our comrades, and my dear little English pony, my saddle and bridle, blanket and camlet cloak, fell into the hands of the enemy.

The only thing that escaped was my little Portuguese boy, who I suppose was valueless. I never saw the pony again, but I heard that she was afterwards seen in the streets of Paris. The next morning there was an auction of all the stores, &c., that we had taken, mules and all. In consideration of the loss of my pony, my general allowed me to get one of the mules at a low price. I selected one which I thought was the best, and got on his back to go and join my company, but before we got out of the street he tumbled on his head, sending me face foremost on to the pavement. I, however, was light, and escaped pretty safe, only a little bruised, but I determined never to perch myself on the back of a mule again. The French army never could make another stand; they retired over the Pass of Maya, where a few days ago they had driven back and killed numbers of our Highland Brigade.

We again marched up to the top of the Pyrenees, and again looked down upon France, and in another day or two found ourselves back in our old position above Roncesvalles, in which town we heard that only a week before Marshal Soult had asked, as he rode through the town, "Where are those redcoats, that I may drive them into the sea." He had not gone far before he found them, and I suspect he found that he had "caught a Tartar."

I must say a few words before taking leave of the beautiful valley of Bastan, after the capture of the convoy destined for the relief of Pampeluna. We pursued the flying French Army in the direction of the Pass of Maya, where the Highland Brigade of our division had so distinguished themselves and suffered so much just a week before. We advanced until we arrived at the summit of the Pyrenees at the Pass of Maya, and again had the satisfaction of looking down upon the "sunny fields of *La Belle France*."

As we ascended the mountain I saw an officer in hot pursuit of a round loaf of bread that was rolling down the mountain at best pace. With great difficulty the officer just overtook it as it arrived near the spot where I was standing. On looking at him I discovered that he was my cousin, William L'Estrange, then a subaltern in the 11th Regiment, the same who afterwards settled at Kilcommon, in the King's County, and became the father of a numerous and interesting family. This was the first and only time I met him during the campaigns, as his regiment was attached to another division of the army.

We were not long kept in suspense on the top of the Pyrenees, and soon received the order to return to Elizondo. We reached it about dusk, and were informed that we were to remain there for the night. The baggage had not come up. My pony, with my blanket and boat-cloak, was a prisoner in France. I was the only officer now with my company, Girdlestone having been again wounded and gone to the rear. I had nothing for it but to select the softest stone I could find for a pillow, and lie down to take my night's repose with nothing but the clothes I had had on me for the last week. Never did I sleep sounder, though I felt the cold of the night air without a covering very severely; nevertheless I never slept sounder in my life, and, as the day dawned, what was my delight in seeing that the baggage had come up, and that it, with Antonio, was just on the opposite side of a small, clear rivulet, on the banks of which I had taken my night's repose.

I was very soon upon my legs, and quickly divested myself of all my clothes, plunged into the river and swam across, congratulating myself on having parted company particularly with my under garments. I sent Antonio round to fetch my upper garments, which I could not afford to part with in the present state of my wardrobe, but desired him to leave the rest on the bank to their fate. On inquiring for my faithful old batman, Tim Ferry, who had been ordered to join the ranks at the commencement of these actions, I was informed that he had received a severe wound in the knee; that in his agony he exclaimed, "Och, I may thank the captain (meaning Captain Dowdale) for this, for if I had been with the baggage I wouldn't have been here!"

This was the last I heard of the poor fellow, and I believe he died of the wound. Having enjoyed the luxury of a change of garments and of clean linen, which I had been for ten days a stranger to, I felt myself so refreshed by my night's repose and my cold bath that I was ready for anything; but when I looked down on my general's shoes that he lent me at Roncesvalles, I said, "How can I think of returning them in this condition? They are not fit to make a pair of old slippers." I did, however, return them, and they were thankfully received by Sir John. We immediately commenced our march to our old quarters at Roncesvalles, where we arrived without any great adventure, and reoccupied the old stations which the French marshal had endeavoured to drive us from, and remained till the opening of the next and final campaign, which included the battles of the Nive, Nivelle, Orthes, and, winding up, the uncalled-for Battle of Toulouse. (It is supposed that Marshal Soult was quite aware that it was all up with the emperor before he fought the Battle of Toulouse).

CHAPTER 5

Crossing the Nive

Three weary months slowly passed away after the excitement of the last battle in the Pyrenees. Nothing could be more monotonous than our lives: we reoccupied our old camp; we had nothing to excite or employ us. All fear of attack from the front had vanished. Even the emperor's lieutenant, Marshal Soult, with all his energy and soldierly qualities, could not again organize an army to take the offensive.

When we strolled out on the fields in which we had been so hotly engaged fighting so short a time since, nothing remained but the little mounds of earth hastily thrown over the dead, but so lightly, that in many instances an arm, a foot, or perhaps a leg was exposed: and a hideous stench polluted and infected the air near these scattered graves. These were but melancholy promenades. The bodies, we knew, had all been stripped, for even the lofty tops of the mountain where they fell did not protect the dead from the heartless and often murderous camp-followers, whose trade it is to rifle the dead of their clothing, and it must be feared not unfrequently shortening the term of the mortal suffering of the wounded who have the misfortune to fall into their merciless hands.

I can scarcely recall to my *Recollections* the manner in which we passed this uninteresting period. We had ample time to discuss the various scenes of danger and bloody strife through which we had passed; to recall to memory and lament the friends we had lost, and talk over their noble deeds and their failures; and those who smoked—of whom in those days I was not one—puffed their pipes or cigars, by way of passing their time; until at length came the month of November, with a snowstorm which I shall never forget.

Our camp equipage, and especially our tents, had come out from England at the beginning of the year; they had therefore been a long time in store, and consequently the tent-cloths were rather decayed, which was unpleasant indeed, for when the snow begins to fall on the top of the Pyrenees it comes with a vengeance. I fancied myself very comfortable in my tent, with a stretcher and mattress, under a pair of blankets, when, about the middle of the night, or towards the morning, I felt something uncommonly heavy, very wet and cold, descend upon me. I was for some time in doubt of what had happened, and half asleep, half awake, knew not what to do.

The snow had fallen very heavily on the tent, and a sudden gust of wind, added to the weight of the snow, had forced the pole of the tent through the top of it. I did not exactly like my position, and with considerable difficulty crawled from under the debris, and sought shelter in a neighbouring tent belonging to a brother officer, and having ensconced myself, as I thought, comfortably in my blankets, which I had managed to bring with me, fancied I was all snug again. I had not, however, been more than ten minutes in my new quarters, when an exactly similar catastrophe occurred. I therefore gave up, as hopeless, making any improvement in my condition for that night, beyond a partial propping up; and when I arose in the morning, and looked out, there was scarcely a single tent in the camp standing.

Our position now became untenable; we were not long kept in suspense; our good general, Sir John Byng, soon heard of the position we were in, and early in the morning we were greeted by an order to descend immediately to Roncesvalles. We were alert in obeying this order, and reached the bottom of the hill before nightfall. There we found our battalion under the command of that gallant Scotchman, Colonel, afterwards Sir James Leith. The 31st was about the only regiment which carried on the appearance of a mess during the campaign. It consisted of the field officers, the captains, the Adjutant Bolton, Lieutenant Elwyn (an exceedingly well-informed English gentleman), and myself.

When the light companies returned from their elevated perch, we found a sort of mess-room erected of branches of trees, and covered with the fresh skins of the animals lately slaughtered for our rations; these made a tolerable roof as long as the fine weather lasted, but when two or three feet of snow rested on this roof, the internal heat from the dinner-party, the dinner, and the cigars, which were constantly burning, naturally melted the snow on the top of the fresh sheep or goatskins, and a ruddy drop kept perpetually falling into our *potage* or our glasses of grog.

Tents in a snowstorm.

I thought this might be a good time to try what game there was to be shot, particularly as I heard the note of the wild goose, as I lay in my bed one moonlight night, passing very near over our heads on their migratory southern passage. I was rather disappointed not seeing one after a long walk with my gun the next day; but I got a shot at a woodcock, and bagged him, and, on examination, I found that he had lost a leg either by shot or trap; but the wound was perfectly healed, and must have happened in the previous season at latest. It was impossible that we could remain much longer in this position. A report was current that an outlying picket had been lost in the snowstorm, and I believe there was a life or two lost. At all events, we were obliged to abandon a couple of our field-pieces on the summit of the mountain; the snow totally prevented their removal.

The next morning our general received orders to move to the left, in the direction of the valley of the Bastan. We made an early start, and had much difficulty in making our way through the almost impervious, wooded mountain side, upon mere goatherds' pathways; but, after a march of six or eight hours, we had descended out of the region of snow, and found the weather very pleasant, though cold; this was, I think, upon the 9th of November. We reached the valley towards nightfall, close to the Maya Pass; the moon was at the full, and really as bright as day. We then had a night-march, crossed over the summit of the pass, and began to descend into the territory of the enemy.

Our generals knew well that the French Army occupied an entrenched camp in our front. It was an important point that it should not be discovered that we were descending on them. The bright shining of the muskets, which, though called "Brown Bess," were as bright as steel, or the large brass plates worn in those days in front of the soldiers' caps, might betray us to the enemy on that bright night. Our men were therefore ordered to turn the brass plates on their caps to the rear and to reverse their arms, and march as silently as possible; the battle of the Nive was before us.

Early in the morning Lord Hill's *corps d'armée* formed in close columns at the French foot of the Pyrenees. It was a sight to be remembered. "We were going to carry the war into the heart of the enemy's country; in fact, to invade the so long overbearing country, the mighty French Empire, with its still unvanquished emperor at its head, and still in command of enormous armies. His first general (Soult) he had appointed his lieutenant, and placed him at the head of what remained of the army of Spain; and nobly did he do his duty to his emperor and his country. Defeated time after time, his army dispersed and fugitive, he rallied them in a most wonderful manner, and fought the four last general actions of the campaign and several minor ones with consummate ability and courage.

Shortly after daybreak, on the 10th of November, Sir Rowland Hill's fine corps marched past, the officers saluting, and we soon heard distant firing on the left, and could see the flashes from the artillery and musketry by degrees it advanced nearer, and we could observe that the French army, notwithstanding their entrenched position, were being driven back. The position occupied by the French was a low range of hills, the left of the French Army resting behind their entrenchments exactly in our front; and very soon the left of the British Army had established themselves on the position abandoned by the French, and were rapidly advancing towards the front of our division, and, taking the French on their flank, were apparently gaining an easy victory; the French seemed unable to resist them.

Our general of division (Sir William Steward) apparently feared that the victory would be gained without his assistance, and that our names would not be mentioned in the despatch. At all events he gave orders to us to advance and attack that part of the French position in our front. Rather fearful loss of life ensued. The Frenchmen were posted behind a deep trench, the bank being thrown up on their side of the ditch. This gave them great protection; and, besides this, about one hundred yards in their front, they had cut down trees and placed other obstacles, forming an abatis, through which we had to approach them almost in single files, and the consequence was that our men were shot down almost as fast as they emerged, like woodcocks from their cover.

The cannon-balls were passing over our heads from both sides, and in less than ten or fifteen minutes the ground was covered with our killed and wounded; how I escaped is a marvel to me to the present day. My captain, however—poor Girdlestone, who had only just rejoined us from the rear, recovered from his second wound in the Pyrenees—was again severely wounded. His left arm was so shattered that he wore it in a leather case for the rest of his life; it would have been better if it had been amputated on the spot. I never saw him but once afterwards in London, his arm still suspended in its leather case. A braver soldier never stepped, or a more perfect gentleman.

Several other officers and men fell in this short but sanguinary encounter. How I reached the ditch and got over it I cannot say, the moment was too exciting for *Recollections*; but I did get over with a very few of my men, and thought it my duty, in the absence of any orders—for I was again my own commanding officer—to advance after the retiring French, trusting to being followed by what remained of my gallant light company. As I proceeded I saw a French soldier, who, in the act of running away, turned and fired his musket. He was then about a couple of hundred yards before. I suddenly felt a blow in the upper part of my leg that astonished me. I had heard that a wound at first did not inflict much pain; I found it quite the reverse with a contusion, for I felt it very sorely, clapped my hand on my thigh, and expected to see it covered with blood; but no, it was only a severe contusion, breaking the skin on the spot it had struck, the mark of which I still retain, and my leg was next day black from my knee to my hip.

At the very moment I received the blow a mounted officer rode up to me and said, "Hallo, George, are you much hurt?" It was my before-mentioned cousin Edmund, then *aide-de-camp* to Sir Denis Pack, whose division it was that was chasing the French before them, and would soon have cleared our front had our general had the patience to wait for them. Edmund put his hand into his holster and produced a sandwich, which he gave me.

I said to him, "There is the rascal that fired the shot that hit me," pointing to a Frenchman some distance in our front.

He put spurs to his horse and went at best speed after him, and soon came up to him; the Frenchman in the meantime had time to reload. As Edmund came up to him, he turned round and fired his musket in his face. Edmund rode leisurely back to me and said, "That fellow will never fire at you again." He had cut him down; but he said, "Look here;" the whole of the front of his cocked hat which the staff wore in those days, fore and aft, was blown off, and singed with the powder of the Frenchman's musket—a close shave rather.

We continued to advance, and passing by the rows of French huts, which were built in regular line, I went into one of them from curiosity. I had a pair of white Russian ducks on, and when I came out of the hut I looked down and saw the lower part of my ducks perfectly black. They were covered with fleas, with which the huts abounded. We proceeded in our advance until we arrived at a sort of *tête-de-pont*. The bridge, however, was blown up, and the French army, with several pieces of artillery, was on the other side. This was the bridge of Cambo, so well known to many of our officers.

A sort of cannonade was kept up from both sides until the evening closed in, and we of course halted for the night, and tried to make ourselves as comfortable as possible, and await the events of the coming day with as much patience as we could command. Amongst those who fell, killed, and were wounded of my acquaintance on this eventful morning, besides Girdlestone's severe wound, Major Acland of the 57th, or old "Die-Hards," who had lately been attached to our light companies, died a soldier's death. He was greatly lamented.

The next morning at dawn we were all on the alert; with a swollen river in our front (the Nive), the remains of the blown-up bridge upon it, a very deep ford just above the broken bridge, and a French Army on the other side, it looked as if we should have something very sharp. We knew that our artillery could keep clear a certain distance from the bridge and the banks of the river, and we advanced with the usual confidence of British soldiers.

When we came up to the river it looked formidable enough; a strong stream running, and we did not exactly know the depth of the ford. Mine was the leading company. My general, Byng, desired me to wade before the company descended into it, to prove its depth. I of course obeyed his orders, and found that it took me up to the hips, and thanked my stars when I reached the other side without a volley from our opposite friends, which I fully expected, or even a cannon-shot thrown at us. The fact was, the French had retreated. My company, with their pouches over their knapsacks, to "keep their powder dry," followed by threes, their arms linked for mutual support, and soon stood by my side.

The rest of the division quickly followed, but it was remarkable how much the resistance of so many men in the water increased its force and raised its height, so that they were all pretty well soused: some were carried away by the stream, especially the Portuguese, who do not appear to be good waders; and I even saw a dragoon, horse and all, carried down by the torrent, and I conclude they were drowned, though we did not wait to see the result. Being the first to cross, I believe I suffered less from the ducking than the rest of the brigade; and I know on rather a cold day I took a long time to dry, but felt myself considerably warmer from our rapid march; and when we arrived at the pretty village of Vieux Mouguerre, I shortly afterwards saw some magnificent hogs slaughtered, the hair burnt or singed off by straw fires, and served out to us for rations. I thought I had never eaten such delicious pork-chops in my life before.

We were now close to the celebrated fortress of Bayonne, just out of the reach of the guns, and I shall later have to relate what fighting happened in and about that town, caused by the repeated gallant though unsuccessful sorties made by Marshal Soult on the left, and afterwards on the right flank of the British Army.

"We got into rather comfortable quarters at Vieux Mouguerre; at all events we had a roof over our heads—a desirable substitute for our old tents on the mountains, of which we had become tired. Sir John Byng established himself in a very good house at the Bayonne extremity of the town, belonging probably to the lord or squire of the village, and Sir Rowland Hill occupied a tolerably good house in the village, where he also put up his pack of hounds. Our little mess was placed on the best footing possible, and one of the deserters who joined our regiment in the Pyrenees became our messman, and, considering his knowledge of the country and French customs, it was judicious our appointing him.

We had not many duties to interfere with our amusements, which were chiefly shooting-parties, though we were not rewarded with any great amount of game. I generally carried my gun on my shoulder in case of a chance shot. The most unpleasant part of our duty was the standing-to-arms an hour before daylight, and remaining there till we could see a grey horse a mile off. We had also unpleasant night pickets on the bank of the river Adour on our right, by which river provisions, &c., were conveyed into Bayonne in boats; these always moved at night with muffled oars, and our duty was to fire into them as they passed, if we could find out in what direction to take our aim; but we could seldom ascertain whether our fire had produced effect; the river was wide and rapid, and the nights were very dark. We had also another unpleasant duty, which was the outlying pickets about a mile from the town in the direction of Bayonne, and of course kept up communication with those in the rear, in case of any alarm from the front.

Nearly a month passed away very speedily, and the middle of December was reached, during which period the French marshal, Soult, was indefatigable in reorganising the remains of the French army, raising recruits and reinforcements in every possible way. The British army was cut in two by a considerable river, the Nive. Lord Wellington's left rested on the sea, his right upon the above-named river. Lord Hill's corps and another division lay between two rivers, the Nive and Adour; the right, being our brigade, was protected by the river I have before designated, the Adour.

Here was a fine opportunity for Soult attacking our army in detail, which he was not long in availing himself of. He moved the right of his army through Bayonne, and commenced a furious assault on the British left, but after a severe conflict the French were defeated. We could plainly hear the guns and the firing during this action. But though Soult was defeated, he did not despair.

On the night of the 12th of December I was in command of the most advanced outlying picket, not very far from the walls of Bayonne. I was very much on the alert, as I felt I was in a responsible position, and took no rest that night, for I heard a rumbling noise going on during the whole period, from the movement, it appeared to me, of guns and waggons through the strongly-fortified town. So convinced was I that there was something in the wind, that I sent my corporal to say what I had observed and heard, and to communicate the intelligence at the proper quarter in the rear. Nor was I mistaken; the marshal had moved nearly the whole of his army through Bayonne in the night, and the first ray of light in the morning assured me that an attack was meditated.

Shortly after daylight our pickets were called in, and very shortly afterwards a tremendous attack was made on our portion of the army, and never did that army distinguish itself more than in repelling so gloriously this assault. The French came on in heavy column; Sir John Byng had moved his brigade to the left, leaving the light companies and some other troops to defend that part of the position in front of Vieux Mouguerre. We had some very sharp practice, and, overwhelmed with numbers, were driven through the greater part of the village.

Sir John Byng's brigade stood the brunt of this part of the action and highly distinguished itself, particularly by a charge they made on the heavy attacking columns, when he took the king's colour out of the hands of Elwyn who carried it, and headed the charge, for which he has now the colour of the 31st in his armorial bearings and the words "Vieux Mouguerre," and as supporters two soldiers of the grenadier company of the 31st.

Poor Elwyn, who was a very sensitive man, felt this very much, and, as I heard, shed tears, for I was to the right; it would have been my duty to have carried the king's colour as junior lieutenant, had I not been detached with my own light company. Elwyn, who, as I have already said, was a very high-minded and accomplished officer, as brave and bold as a lion, felt it was a sort of slur on his courage; but no other officer or soldier in the brigade had any other opinion of him than that he was everything a soldier ought to be. I am very glad to have this opportunity of speaking of him, though in after-life I never met him; and as he was of rather a delicate constitution, he probably did not live very long; and if he has departed this life, which is only too probable, his friends may not object to the liberty I have taken of sounding his praise.

While our brigade was so warmly engaged with the enemy, Colonel Ross's troop of horse artillery arrived at a most opportune moment; nothing could exceed the gallant style in which they went into action; the celerity of their movement, the admirably well-directed fire which they threw into the French column contributed in a great degree to the signal victory we obtained. The French were now again defeated, and retired in the best order they could under the walls of Bayonne. We advanced until our skirmishers were almost mixed together.

My little light company occupied a grove of tall elm-trees, which were some protection; for not only musketry, but shot and shell were crashing through the trees over and about us. I found that my men had exhausted all their ammunition. I went up to Major Cameron, of the Buffs, who commanded us, to tell him so, and that I saw French soldiers in the wood close to us, and what were we to do?

"Give them the bayonet if they come on," said the major.

"Very well, sir," said I, and returned to my company.

At the foot of the tree I was standing by, I saw one of my company lying oh his back; I stood over him, and saw him raise his arm, and put his hand to the back of his head; he did this several times, but I saw at once it was all over with him, a musket-ball having entered his forehead and come out at the back, a fearful wound. I then recognised that it was the body of poor McMulty, a man from the county of Sligo, but not one of my original volunteers. I felt very sorry for the poor fellow; he was as brave a soldier as ever walked, and had been all through the war.

The only difficulty in action was to restrain him, for he was always pushing himself into danger; and when, on one occasion, I remonstrated with him, and told him he would be surely shot, "Oh, sir," he said, "they will never kill me until I have my pockets full of Frenchmen's gold." A prophecy which was nearly accomplished, for he showed me a watch which he got from a dead Frenchman at Vittoria, and I believe he also got some *doubloons*, which he did not acknowledge. His great fault was that it was very hard to keep him in order in quarters; he was a very determined fellow, and could not resist the temptation of rum, or still greater, of what is called loot. I was, however, sorry to lose such a man from my now sadly diminished company.

Very shortly before this action, a day or two only, a youth joined the Buffs, just sent out from England. I cannot resist mentioning his name, for, though our acquaintance was short, I took a great fancy to him—his name was Blake. I think he came from Norfolk, and when he joined he was appointed to a vacancy in the light company of that gallant old corps, the Buffs. He was very tall, remarkably handsome, well dressed, and evidently a gentleman every inch of him. What was my dismay to see him also stretched on his back in the same wood. I went up to him, and found a cannon-shot had passed through both his thighs. He was carried into Vieux Mouguerre, and amputation was performed by a surgeon of his regiment that night, which he bore like a hero; and I heard that he recovered from his very severe wound; and though he lived some time after, I never saw him again, save once, when I went in to ask him how he was after his amputation. I cannot say how much I felt for this poor young gentleman. Night brought the action to a close. We returned into our old quarters, and refreshed ourselves as we could after this hard day, and waited impatiently the English newspapers, with Lord Wellington's despatch, giving an account of these actions.

CHAPTER 6

The Advance into France

Very shortly after this a general order came out from Lord Wellington's headquarters, which caused some sensation in the army at the time. The commanding officers of three regiments in our division were given leave to return to England. The regiments were the Buffs, the 71st, and the "Die-Hards," or 57th Regiment.

It was easy to account for two of these being sent home, the officers commanding the Buffs and the 71st. Our general had met one of them going to the rear during the action, and on asking him where he was going to, he said he was going to the rear to order up ammunition.

The 71st Regiment, commanded by the other, had become much demoralised since the death of their celebrated colonel (Cadogan) at Vittoria; but why was old McDonald, of the "Die-Hards," included in this order? He certainly had one misfortune—he had grown too old in the service, and perhaps it was time that he should be relieved from duty—but he was as hard as nails, as full of fight as any Irishman or Scotchman, and he was highly respected, I may say adored, in his regiment; and we all felt hurt, and he, I believe, more than any of us, that his name appeared in such company. I believe he did not long survive it. Though I recollect the names of the other two, I do not, after what I have just said, wish to make them public, and perhaps wound the feelings of their relatives, if they have any left.

We remained peacefully and unmolested for a considerable time at Vieux Mouguerre after the actions. My general was very kind to me, and often had me to dinner at his villa. Between that and Bayonne was a very woodcock looking piece of cover, which I had a great hankering after. One day, strolling out with my gun on my shoulder, a gentleman in a blue frock-coat and round hat, was riding past, when he asked me if I could tell him where General Hill resided in this village.

Though I had scarcely ever seen him before, I could not be mistaken in those marked features and eagle-eye. I said, "Oh, my lord, I shall be happy to show you!" It was Lord Wellington himself. I walked beside his horse and pointed out the house he inquired for, when he thanked me, and left me as proud as a peacock after having a conversation with our great commander. He did not remain more than half an hour or so. I hung about the town in hopes of seeing him again, and shortly after his departure Sir Rowland Hill came riding by with his pack of hounds at his heels. With his invariably kind and almost bashful manner, he said, "I am going to put my hounds into this little wood; they may perhaps flush a woodcock, and you get a shot."

This was exactly the thing I longed for, and feeling elated by being spoken to by the two great men of the army, I followed the hounds to the cover-side; but, alas! no woodcock made its appearance, to my no small disappointment.

Shortly after this my cousin Edmund, whom I have often mentioned, rode into our village, called on me, and said his division (the 6th) was within a few miles: "You must come over and dine with my general (Pack), and we will make you a shakedown for the night." I lost no time in going to our colonel (Leith) to ask his permission; and, though rather rough, there was not a warmer-hearted fellow in the army. He at once gave me permission to go, and I ordered out my steed, who had actually grown fat and sleek on the bruised goss or furzes, which was nearly his only forage, and which abounds in that district. Edmund and I started for General Pack's headquarters; he received me cordially, and soon put me at my ease. We had a good dinner and a pleasant party.

The officers on his staff were particularly conspicuous by their extremely handsome appearance and their splendid Hussar uniforms that of the 10th Hussars, at that time the crack cavalry regiment of the army. Their names were the Count de Grammont and Captain Synge. I never saw two finer specimens of what a soldier ought to be—magnificent-looking fellows; the count, I believe, afterwards became Duc de Guise. I often saw Colonel Synge in Ireland afterwards. They quite eclipsed my little cousin Edmund L'Estrange, an especial favourite with Pack, (see appendix), who left a written record of his worth, which was sent to me afterwards by his successor, and which I still preserve. After looking over the field of action and the particular points and circumstances, and listening to a detail of what took place from Edmund, I returned to my old quarters and companions, rather

SIR GEORGE MEETING THE DUKE ON HORSEBACK.

proud of the distinguished individuals I had been visiting.

There was a considerable lull in our warlike operations after these severe and sanguinary actions. We had no apprehension from the front; we knew the French Army had pretty nearly had enough of it, and were not likely to renew the contest or be the assailants.

The English newspapers began to bring tidings from the great emperor's army in the north of Europe, of disasters in Russia, of the burning of Moscow, and the commencement of that sad and fearful retreat. Discomfited by Russia, France lay before us. The so frequently defeated army which had occupied Spain, notwithstanding the exertions made by their newly-arrived general, Field-Marshal Soult, was dispirited. Our troops had gained so much confidence in their commander and the gallant generals in command of divisions and brigades that they were irresistible.

The Spaniards themselves were reorganised, clothed, and equipped by British capital, and now presented a formidable and efficient force; but their hatred to France, their irrepressible tendency to plunder the country, drew forth the most stringent orders from the commander-in-chief, who was forced to keep them very much in check and towards the rear, lest their atrocities should rouse the French nation against us; our commander's game being to gain them to our side, which they showed they were well disposed to. Very severe notice was taken of any act of plunder on the part of our own men; and I recollect an order, written on half a sheet of paper, with reference to two men who had been detected by our commander himself in the act of plunder, *viz*:

> Private so-and-so, of blank regiment, now in charge of the provost-marshal of the second division, will be hanged tomorrow morning, in presence of such troops as can be conveniently assembled.

I saw the order carried into execution.

The winter had now nearly passed away, and the fine weather so peculiar to the South of France seemed to have set in. Our cavalry and the other horses and mules of the army had recovered their condition; reinforcements had come out from England. In fact, we were in prime order to commence another campaign, and in full expectation to receive the order to advance.

Soult was no despicable general, notwithstanding all his reverses, and was full of resources. The order at length came to move. A strong detachment of the army was left in the rear to blockade Bayonne. The commander of that fortress we knew would defend it to the last, which he did, and made his celebrated and sanguinary sortie, when the Guards lost so many brave officers and men, when the war had virtually come to an end, and after the battle of Toulouse. Our army started in a southern direction towards Tarbes and Pau. We had to cross several of the gaves or streams that descend from the Pyrenees. We had as yet not seen the face of our enemy, but we knew they were not far off.

As we approached Tarbes an order was passed, "Cavalry to the front." In a short time a brigade of light dragoons came rattling past us at a great pace, their sabres drawn, and evidently eager for the fray. We drew up on one side of the narrow road to give them room to pass, and were not a little splashed by the mud they threw up as they went by. I heard a soldier remark to his comrade, "Never mind, they will soon come back again," an observation which was very soon fulfilled, as the order for "Infantry to the front," was passed, and we soon went by the cavalry again. The ground was not fit for cavalry action, and after some slight skirmishing, in which our light cavalry showed that they were ready for anything, we advanced to the front, but found that the enemy had "skedaddled," to use a Yankee expression.

Our next march was then to the charming little town of Pau, situated in a lovely country with its beautifully-trained vineyards. We would willingly have halted here for a few days, to enjoy the delights of what is now become such a fashionable watering-place, but that was not our destiny; *en avant* was the word of the British Army, and we at once commenced our advance. At the end of a long day's march, late in the evening, we came into what appeared an admirable bivouac, plenty of wood and water, and our baggage well up. Just as we reached the camping-ground I saw a woodcock, and thought I marked him down. I lost no time in communicating this important piece of information to my friend and chum and invariable shooting companion, Stepney St. George, of the 66th.

We lost not a minute in getting our guns together and proceeding in pursuit of our doomed game. We had not an idea that there was a Frenchman within five miles of us; but just as we got to the spot where I expected to find the woodcock, we heard the bugles of the brigade sounding the assembly. We of course hurried back to our respective regiments, and just arrived in time to fall into our places when we were ordered to advance. A terrible sharp piece of work we had of it. Exactly in our front was a hill of considerable height, sparingly covered with trees and very steep, on the top of which was a division of the French army, under the command of General Harispe. They had just come up from Barcelona, where they had only to contend with the troops of Sir John Murray, and did not know what it was to get the worst of it.

In less than fifteen minutes after leaving our camp we found ourselves hotly engaged with this new corps. They stood their ground like men, and even crossed bayonets with a battalion of our division, which I think was the 39th, in General O'Callaghan's brigade. This, though one of the shortest, was one of the most sanguinary actions of the campaign. It was not what is called a general action, but was styled the Battle of Garris. When I got to the top of the hill it was so dark that I could scarcely discern whether the stems of the trees were not Frenchmen. Just at the point at which we arrived was a single, solitary-looking house, which none of us had the time or curiosity to look into.

I was in the front of this house, looking towards where the enemy ought to be, and trying to form my scattered company. I had just moved from the left flank to the right, when I saw a rush of soldiers. They were a party of twenty or thirty Frenchmen, who had concealed themselves in this house, and, in the dusk, made a rush down and wounded the left-hand man of my company. We managed, however, to give them a parting volley as they rushed down the hill, but whether with effect I never ascertained or went to look. I forgot to mention that after the battles near Bayonne, &c., I was considered too young an officer to be left in command of the light company, and Captain Edward Knox was appointed to it. On this evening poor Knox received a severe wound through the shoulder blade-bone, and it was found necessary to take the arm out at the socket. I frequently met him in after-life. He was an excellent good fellow, and could do more with his one arm that was left than most people could do with two. The command of the company was not taken from me again until the end of the war.

My poor shooting companion and great friend, Stepney St. George, came to great grief on this eventful evening. As I said before, being always well mounted, he generally acted as *aide-de-camp* when we were engaged. How he managed to ride up this steep hill I cannot conceive, but he did so. Just as he arrived at the summit he received a musket-ball in his left arm, and, as he fell from his horse, his head came in contact with the point of the bayonet of one of his own men, which pierced his skull: for this he was afterwards trepanned when he came to England. He was carried down by bullock-waggon to Cambo, where there was an hospital, and he has often related to me the miseries and the torture he underwent: his recovery was miraculous. He did, however, recover, and afterwards married my youngest sister, by whom he left a large family.

Another fine fellow also fell in this action, Colonel Fearon, a brother of our lieutenant-colonel. He commanded a fine battalion of Portuguese in the brigade of that noble fellow Sir John Buchan, who was a most intimate and kind friend of mine. We remained on the field that night, and made the best of it, but it was uncomfortable enough. The next day we moved in the direction of Orthes, where the celebrated battle was on the eve of coming off.

CHAPTER 7

Towards Toulouse

The short, very sharp, and decisive action on the heights of Garris, with which my last chapter concluded, was no impediment to our immediate advance, and towards the middle of the next day we were in motion in the direction of Orthes, and it was not very long before we were within sound of the booming of the great guns. Lord Wellington had again brought Marshal Soult and the French army to bay. The attack commenced on the left, and though the enemy made a very determined stand at the commencement, they were totally unable to resist the impetuous attack made on them by the divisions composing the left of the British army, in which, however, we suffered severe loss; and amongst those severely wounded was the late Duke of Richmond, then Lord March, who received a musket-ball through the body.

He was on the staff of Lord Wellington and in the 52nd Light Infantry, the uniform of which was almost identical with that which I wore—that of the Light Infantry of the 31st Regiment—and I was on more than one occasion spoken to in mistake for him. We had been at Westminster together, and I well remember how he led on his schoolfellows in repelling the attacks that in those days were annually made by the roughs in Tothill Street and its then discreditable neighbourhood on the Westminster Boys on and after the celebrated 5th of November. Though His Grace recovered from his severe wound, I have heard that he felt it occasionally for the rest of his life; but he lived to obtain the tardy Peninsular medal for that gallant army, though nearly thirty years elapsed from the period when it was won. I got one of the medals with six clasps, and was at the dinner given to the Duke of Richmond on the occasion, which was attended by 200 officers, of which I was the youngest in the room.

When our corps (Sir Rowland Hill's) came in sight of the field at Orthes the battle had been virtually gained. We saw the greater part of the French army scattered over the plain like a flock of sheep in full retreat, or rather running away, throwing down their knapsacks, their muskets, and everything that could impede their flight, for such it must be called, and all moving in an oblique direction from the left towards our right, in the hope of gaining a certain bridge, where they expected they would be safe. "Where are the cavalry?" everybody asked. "What an opportunity they are losing of going into these runaways and making a clean sweep of them!" But the cavalry at that moment were not available, and most of the fugitives gained the desired bridge.

We thought that the French Army must be so demoralised by this defeat, that it would be no easy matter to again get them into fighting order; but the French marshal was not so easily extinguished, and before many days he was able again to show a front; and at St. Gauden's, and afterwards at Aire, we had some sharp fighting, but always with the advantage on our side. After a sharp action near Aire, where our division was engaged, towards evening, as darkness approached, our light company's commander, Major Daniel Dudgeon, of the 66th, a man weighing twenty stone, who rode a black charger seventeen hands high, from which he had alighted, told me that my company must furnish an outlying picket.

"Very well, major," said I; "I'll go."

Then he said he would accompany me to place the picket; so we advanced through a narrow lane up to our ankles in mud and water, for there had been heavy rain, and I followed the big major. We had not advanced very far when I saw a flash from a musket in front, for it was now nearly dark, and I saw my dear old commandant fall down in the muddy lane and splash me all over. I immediately, with the help of a few soldiers, got him lifted up, and we carried him into a small house that happened to be near.

We lost no time in sending for the surgeon of the regiment, who soon arrived, and we laid poor Dudgeon down on a table in the room. We discovered that a ball had entered at the stomach—a very corpulent and aldermanic one—and it struck me that it must be all up with him. The surgeon, however, continued his examination, and at last said, "I think I feel the ball." He took his lancet, made a slight incision in his back, and held the ball in his hand. We of course thought it had passed through his body; but no, this was not the case. It had struck on a very elastic substance, had passed all round his body just under the skin, and lodged in his back, from which it was extracted as related; and many months had not elapsed before we had the dear old man back again with us, to the great delight of his numerous friends and admirers, for he was a favourite with all.

When he was taken to the rear I began to look about my outlying picket. The fires of the French Army were blazing on every hill as far as the eye could carry us, and I watched them with great interest, speculating upon whether they would wait for us or give us another field day the next morning. The practised eye soon learns to discover signs and tokens. I watched the night-fires, and could distinguish when men passed to and fro between me and the fire.

For a long period I could see that they were there; but towards morning the fires began to decline, I could see no passing to and fro, and I came to the conclusion that they were off, turned into the small house, where the operation had been performed on Dudgeon, and slept soundly till the bugle sounded in the morning. Lord Wellington lost no time in following up the retreating French army, which was falling back upon Toulouse. Soult made his final, and as it afterwards turned out, his uncalled for stand; for it was generally understood and believed, that he had received positive and authentic information of the overthrow and downfall of the Great Emperor, and the advance of the allied armies on Paris. He could not resist the temptation of the chance of for once defeating the British Army and their renowned general, in the very strong position he had taken up at Toulouse. He issued a very inflated proclamation to the French Army and people, of which the following is a translation:—

From General Quarters,
8th March, 1814.

Soldiers,—At the Battle of Orthes you did your duty; the enemy suffered much heavier losses than ours; his blood covered the ground; therefore you may consider this passage of arms as an advantage. We are Called to a hundred other combats; there is no repose for us, attacking or attacked, until this army, formed of such extraordinary elements, shall be entirely destroyed, or shall have evacuated the territory of the Empire. However great their numerical superiority, or whatever may be their projects, they little suspect the dangers with which they are surrounded, or the perils which await them; but time will teach them, and also the general who commands them, that French honour cannot be outraged without punishment.

Soldiers!! the general who commands the army against which we fight daily, has had the impudence to incite you, and to incite your countrymen, to revolt and sedition. He speaks of peace, and he excites the French to civil war; thanks to him for letting you know his projects. From that moment your strength is multiplied a hundredfold; from that moment he himself rallied to the Imperial eagles those who by deceptive appearances he had deceived into thinking he carried on the war with loyalty.

No peace with a nation so disloyal and perfidious; no peace with the English and their auxiliaries until they have evacuated the territory of the Empire. They have dared to insult the national honour; they have had the infamy to excite the French to falsify their oaths, and to perjure themselves *vis-à-vis* of the emperor. This offence can only be revenged by blood. To arms! this cry is heard throughout the south; there is not a Frenchman who is not bound to avenge, otherwise he abjures his country, and should be counted among her enemies. A few days more and those who believed in the delicacy and sincerity of the English will discover, at their expense, that these artful promises had no other object than to lower and subdue their courage. If today the English pay and affect generosity, tomorrow enormous contributions will be levied which will largely reimburse their outlay.

These pusillanimous creatures, who calculate the sacrifices they will have to make to save their country, will soon discover that the English, by this war, have no other object than to cause France to destroy herself, and to subjugate the French as they have already done the Spanish, the Portuguese, and the Sicilians, and all other people who groan under their domination. The history of the past will present itself to those anti-French who prefer temporary comforts to the safety of their country; and they will see the English excite Frenchmen to cut one another's throats as they did at Quiberon. They will see the English at the head of all the conspiracies, and of all odious schemes, perfidies, and political assassinations, bouleversing all principles of right by the destruction of all great industrial establishments, thus satisfying their insatiable ambition and greediness.

"Does there exist a single point on the globe where they have not destroyed, by seduction of the workmen, or by violence, the factories and mills in which the products might rival or surpass their own? This will be the fate of our manufacturing establishments, if the English obtain their ends.

Soldiers! condemn to eternal disgrace and execration every Frenchman who has favoured in any way the insidious projects of our enemies. Yow also eternal opprobrium, and deny them as Frenchmen, those who can defend themselves, but who avail themselves of specious pretexts to obtain dispensation of their services; and also those who by corruption or indolence receive and conceal deserters instead of driving them back to their ranks. From this moment there is nothing in common between such men and ourselves, and we can safely anticipate that inexorable history will bring down execration on their names to all posterity.

As to us our duty is distinctly traced out: honour and fidelity is our motto; fight to the last against the enemies of our august emperor and our dear France; respect to property and person; pity the misfortune of those who are momentarily subjected to the enemy, and hasten their deliverance; obedience and implacable hatred to traitors and enemies among Frenchmen; war to the death, to those who endeavour to cause divisions among you, and to those cowards who desert the imperial eagles to range themselves under other colours. Let us always bear in mind the fifteen centuries of glory and innumerable triumphs which have illustrated our country; contemplate the prodigious efforts of our great emperor and his signal victories, which will eternalise the French name. Be you worthy of *him*, and we may then leave, without a stain, to our children the heritage which we received from our fathers; and let us die with arms in our hands sooner than survive our honour.

    Signed by the Marshal of the Empire,
        Lieutenant of the Emperor,
            The Marshal Duke of Dalmatia.

    Certified a true copy by the Lieutenant-General of the Staff of the Army,
            The Count Gazan.

While all these events were in progress, the Duc d'Angouleme had arrived at Bordeaux, and the Mayor of Bordeaux had issued a proclamation declaring in favour of the Bourbons, rather prematurely as Lord Wellington considered it, as it placed him in a difficult position:—

> *Le Maire de Bordeaux à ses Concitoyens,*
> *habitans de Bordeaux.*
> *A Bordeaux, ce 12 Mars, 1814.*

Le magistrat paternal de votre ville a été appelé par les plus heureuses circonstances à se rendre l'interprète de vos voeux trop longtemps comprimés, et l'organe de votre intérêt, pour accueillir, en votre nom, le neveu, le gendre de Louis XVI., dont la présence change en alliés des peuples irrités, qui jusqu'à vos portes ont eu le nom d'ennemis.

Déjà, Bordelais, les proclamations, que, dans l'impuissance de la presse, vos plumes impatientes ont multipliés, nous ont rassurés sur les intentions de votre roi et les projects de ses alliés.

Ce n'est pas pour assujettir nos contrées à une domination étrangère que les Anglais, les Espagnols, et les Portugais y apparaissent. Ils se sont réunis dans le midi, comme d'autres peuples au nord, pour détruire le fléau des nations, et le remplacer par un monarque, père du peuple. Ce n'est même que par lui que nous pouvons appaiser le ressentiment d'une nation voisine, centre laquelle nous a lancé le despotisme le plus perfide.

Si je n'avais été convaincu que la présence des Bourbons conduits par leurs généreux alliés devait amener la fin de vos maux, je n'aurais sans doute jamais déserté votre ville; mais j'aurais courbé la tête en silence sous un joug passager. On ne m'eut point vu arborer cette couleur qui présage un gouvernement pur, si l'on ne m'avait garanti que toutes les classes de citoyens jouiront de ces bienfaits que les progrès de l'esprit humain promettaient à notre siècle.

Les mains des Bourbons sont pures du sang Français. Le testament de Louis XVI. à la main, 'ils oublient tout ressentiment;' partout ils proclament et ils prouvent que la tolérance est le premier besoin de leurs âmes. Instruits que les ministres d'une religion différente de celle qu'ils professent ont gémi sur le sort des rois et des pontifes, ils promittent une égale protection à tous les cultes qui invoquent un Dieu de paix et de réconciliation.

C'est en déplorant des horrible ravages de la tyrannie qu'amena la licence, qu'ils oublient les erreurs causées par les illusions de la liberté. Loin d'en vouloir à ceux qui, avec une ardeur trop punie, en ont pour-

suivi de vains fantômes, ils viennent leur restituer cette liberté véritable qui laisse à la fois le peuple et le monarque sans défiance. Toutes les institutions libérales seront maintenues. Effrayé de la facilité des Français à voter des impôts, soutiens du despotisme, le prince sera le premier à concerter, avec vos représentans, le mode le plus égal, la répartition la plus équitable, pour que le peuple ne soit pas foulé.

Ces courtes et consolantes paroles qui vient de vous adresser l'époux de la fille de Louis XVI. 'Plus de tyran! Plus de guerre! Plus de conscription! Plus de impôts vexatoires!' ont déjà rassuré vos families.

Déjà sa Majesté a deux fois proclamé à la face de l'Europe que l'intérêt de l'état lui ferait une loi de consolider des ventes qui par d'innombrables mutations ont interessé tant de families a des propriétés désormais garanties.

Bordelais! Je me suis assuré que la ferme volont de sa Majesté était de favoriser l'industrie et de ramener parmi nous cette impartiale liberté de commerce qui, avant 1789, avait répandu l'aisance dans toutes les classes laboreuses; vos récoltes vont cesser d'être ruineuses; les colonies trop longtemps séparées de la mere-patrie vous seront rendues; la mer, qui était devenue comme inutile pour vous, va ramener dans votre port des pavilions amis. L'ouvrier laborieux ne verra plus ses mains oisives, et le marin rendu à sa noble profession va naviguer de nouveau pour acheter le repos de sa vieillesse et léguer son expérience à ses fils.

L'époux de la fille de Louis XVI. est dans vos murs: il vous fera bientôt entendre luimême l'expression des sentimens qui l'animent, et de ceux du monarque dont il est le représentant et l'interprète. L'espoir des jours de bonheur qu'il vous assure a soutenu mes forces.

Je n'ai pas besoin de vous inviter à la Concorde. Tous nos voeux ne tendent-ils pas au même but, la destruction de la tyrannic sous laquelle nous avons tous également gémi? Mais chacun de nous doit y concourir avec autant d'ordre que d'ardeur. Amsterdam n'a point attendu la présence de ses libérateurs, pour se prononcer et rétablir l'ancien gouvernement, seul capable de rappeler son commerce et sa prosperité; c'est au patriotisme des négocians que le stadthouder a dû son rétablissement, et la prompte création de l'armée, qui défend par ses mains la liberté Hollandaise.

Les premiers vous aurez donné un semblable exemple à la France. La gloire et l'avantage qu'en retirera notre ville la rendront à jamais célèbre et heureuse entre les cités.

Tout nous permet d'espérer qu'à l'excés des maux vont succéder enfin ces temps désirés par la sagesse, où doivent cesser les rivalités des *nations; et peut-être était-il reservé au Grand Capitaine, qui a déjà mérité le titre de 'Libérateur des Peuples,' d'attacher son nom glorieux à l'époque de cet heureux prodige.*

Tels sont, O mes concitoyens! les motifs, les espérances, qui ont guidé mes démarches et m'ont déterminé à faire pour vous, s'il le fallait, le sacrifice de ma vie. Dieu m'est témoin que je n'ai eu en vue que le bonheur de notre patrie. Vive le Roi!

Le Maire Lynch.

Our corps of the British Army arrived in the neighbourhood of Toulouse early in April, and it was Lord Wellington's intention to have crossed the Garonne above the town of Toulouse, and Sir Rowland Hill's corps, being on the right of the army, was destined to perform this operation. After remaining a day or two in our camp, an order came that we should approach the river, which we did by a very long night-march, and tiresome enough it was, as all night-marches are; but when we arrived within reach of the river, it was discovered that there were not pontoons sufficient to span the river, and our disappointment was great when we found that we were not destined to give the finishing stroke to this brilliant campaign.

Another fatiguing night-march brought us back to our old camping-ground, and a delay took place while Lord Wellington made dispositions to pass the left of the army across the river *below* the town, a feat which he accomplished with his usual judgment, and which has been detailed in his own despatches and every history of the war. We lay patiently in our camp, though sorely regretting the fate that prevented our taking a more prominent part in the approaching action.

However, on the evening of the 9th of April, there were symptoms of a move, and by daylight the next morning we were in the immediate vicinity of the town. We arrived at a long, straight, and wide road or rather street, for there were houses on both sides of it, and it became necessary to feel our way. My company being as usual at the head of the brigade, my dear old general desired me to cross this road or street, and to desire my company to follow, by twos and threes, to ascertain if any of the enemy were in occupation of the houses on the opposite side. I immediately crossed over, and observed that at some distance to my left the enemy had thrown up a barricade to protect the bridge.

I had got about halfway over before I was observed by the Frenchmen, who immediately commenced to pot at me and my men that were following me. I did not think it would be dignified to accelerate my pace, but arrived at the opposite side uninjured, as well as all my men, and was rejoiced to find, instead of French soldiers, a remarkably nice, well-furnished villa, that had evidently been just vacated, containing a billiard-table, and all the apparatus in good order, ladies' shoes and slippers scattered about, with other portions of ladies' dresses, and in fact it gave one the idea of a very respectable and comfortable residence. Though rather fond of a game of billiards, the view from the windows was too interesting to admit of such amusement. The town of Toulouse was under my eyes, and the heights at the other side occupied by the French Army in position quite in view.

Moreover, the action had commenced, and my whole attention was occupied in observing the progress of the great battle that was raging in our front, while I was in comparative safety, only that it was necessary to keep a sharp lookout upon the parties in our immediate front. The battle raged fast and furious for a very considerable period. The Spaniards, who commenced the attack, were unable to make any impression on the French lines, and were in fact driven back; and it was not until Lord Wellington sent a considerable number of the redcoats to the front, that the tide of the action was turned. Our brave fellows suffered severely, and for a long time I was in despair as to the result; the fire sometimes retiring filled me with dismay, and the advancing fire was very slow and apparently indecisive.

The French columns still occupied the hill, and it was not until near evening that I saw the Congreve Rocket Brigade, I believe for the first time brought into action, sending their hissing, serpentine-looking missiles along the top of the hill into the French columns. They could not stand up against these fearful weapons. I saw that the battle was gained, that the French columns were in retreat, and could not help giving a cheer for the result of this sanguinary and conclusive victory.

It is probable that the two or three days which had been lost about the crossing of the river, forced Lord Wellington to fight the battle of Toulouse on Easter Sunday, of all days in the year, being the 10th of April, 1814. Thus terminated this great and glorious war, and I found that we had accomplished, what in my early start I had contemplated, the driving of the French army out of the Peninsula and across the Pyrenees, and began to be proud of myself in having taken a part, though a very humble one, in these triumphant events.

Lord Wellington being aware that the war was at an end, did not think of following up Soult's army. The marshal must have suffered some remorse of conscience in having sacrificed so many lives unnecessarily; but we must all acknowledge that never was there an army so frequently and invariably beaten as his was, making a more brilliant and gallant stand than did this French Army under their indefatigable general and such adverse circumstances. Our entry and reception in Toulouse was something magnificent; the whole population seemed seized with a sudden passion for the Bourbons and the English. From every window in the town, the white flag, or some other emblem of loyalty, was exhibited in the shape of flags or carpets, in shawls or even sheets.

The theatres were opened and filled with English officers and soldiers and loyal French citizens. "God save the King" and "*Vive Henri Quatre*" were the only songs they would listen to; and whenever any of our great officers appeared, he was received with immense cheering. A great ball was given to them; a certain number of officers only could be invited; I was fortunate enough to get an invitation; and as I had preserved pretty well my Light Infantry jacket, and for which I had got a new pair of chain wings, I looked very smart. When I entered the ballroom, I was dazzled with the brilliancy of the lights, and the assemblage of splendidly-dressed ladies, young and old. The young ladies were all ranged round the room like wallflowers.

Sir Lowry Cole introduced me to several French people very good-naturedly as a cousin of his, which was a feather in the cap of a bashful young subaltern; but when I was told I might ask any young lady in the room I pleased to dance, I was entranced and lost no time in making my selection. I fortunately hit upon a first-rate dancer. A waltz was struck up, which was *then* perfectly new to me, but she twirled me round like a *teetotum* till I became so giddy that I thought the whole room was going round, and when we stopped I nearly fell down upon my face. My partner, however, good-naturedly supported me until I had recovered my stability, but I eschewed the waltz for the rest of that evening.

My regiment had passed through the town, and just before we arrived at some charming suburban villas, where we were to take up our quarters, I was rather startled by a loud cheer and seeing the caps of every soldier in the regiment waving in the air over their heads. "What in the world is the matter?" I inquired, when I was informed that my uncle, the late General Guy Carleton L'Estrange, (see appendix 2), had suddenly appeared on the line of march.

After the Battle of Albuera, where he commanded the 31st Regiment, he certainly distinguished himself by an impromptu manoeuvre which overthrew the Polish lancers, and which is still practised in the old regiment, and called the Albuera manoeuvre. He was promoted to the command of the 26th Regiment, and was stationed at Gibraltar. He could not resist the temptation of witnessing the winding up of the war, and he and his friend, Colonel Alexander Saunderson, of Castle Saunderson, father of the present worthy and distinguished member for Cavan, whom I am proud to call my friend, having provided themselves with good horses, started to ride across Spain, which they accomplished; and the manner in which he was received by his old regiment, who had not seen him for more than two years, is a proof of his popularity as a commanding officer. I naturally felt very proud of it, and ever afterwards he was a good and kind uncle to me.

He afterwards married Miss Sarah Rawson, of that beautiful seat, Nidd Hall, in Yorkshire, and they never lost an opportunity of doing me a kindness, or failed to receive me hospitably into their house; in fact I had no relations to whom I was more sincerely attached, or whose memories I more revere than Uncle Guy and Aunt Sarah. They rest in peace side by side, having died without issue, in the ancient burying-ground of the old family of Rawson at Nidd Hall.

The city of Toulouse was the scene of the most exuberant rejoicings; the theatres were thrown open, and balls, concerts, and dinner parties were the order of the day and night, The arrival of my uncle, then Colonel Guy C. L'Estrange of the 26th Regiment, was a subject of great gratification to me. He got a billet close to where his old regiment, the 31st, was stationed, about a mile on the south side of the city. He and I generally rode into the town every morning, to hear the news and amuse ourselves. We heard that a day was appointed for the Duc d'Angoulême to make a sort of triumphal *entrée* into Toulouse. An enormous cavalcade of British and other officers, numbering several hundreds, rode out to meet His Royal Highness some miles from the town and escort him into it, and I formed one of the numerous escort. His reception was enthusiastic, and the rejoicings were kept up for some days.

Lord Charles Churchill had been appointed *aide-de-camp* to General Byng, but did not remain long with him, and he then did me the honour to offer it to me, and asked me to accompany him to Bordeaux on his way to Paris. Before he left he invited General Kempt, who commanded a brigade, to dine with him; he came, and by some accident he was the only guest, so that it was a trio—the two generals and myself. The conversation, in which, however, I scarcely took a part, turned on military affairs, and I was greatly surprised, and my blood began to boil, at several sarcastic and bitter remarks he made to my general. He was, however, the guest, and General Byng accordingly commanded his temper, which he was not always capable of doing, and took little notice of his sarcasms; I was not sorry when he took his departure.

General Byng asked me if I should be ready in a day or two to start for Bordeaux; I said, certainly; so accordingly mounting a splendid thorough-bred black horse called Sultan, his servant leading another black charger, and I mounted on my Rosinante Knockcrockery, we made an early start one morning without any other escort. My general was not a man of very many words, and we rode along slowly and silently enough. One day on our march he asked me, now that our second battalion would probably be reduced and put upon half-pay, what it was my intention to do.

"Should you like to have a commission in the Guards?"

"Of all things," I replied.

He then said, "The Duke of Gloucester is a great friend of mine, and I will be happy to recommend you, and ask for a commission in his regiment (then the 3rd Foot Guards but now the Scots Fusilier Guards); but I should recommend you not to go into the Guards unless you have 200*l.* a year besides your pay."

I said I would write to my father to tell him of this kind offer, which I did, and soon got an answer that I should have the 200*l.* a year.

After a few days, of rather a dreary inarch, we arrived all right at Bordeaux. The mayor of Bordeaux, whom I have already mentioned, took us into his house, and a very hospitable and agreeable quarter it was. And, to my surprise, I found it was the very house in which my cousin Edmund, so often mentioned heretofore, was put up and concealed when making his escape from Bitche; and they showed me the cupboard where he lay *perdu* on the approach of any suspicious characters. I need not say, for their name proclaims it, that this family were of Irish extraction, which probably accounts for their great kindness and protection of one of their own countrymen.

I remained about a week or ten days in this charming place, enjoying the society which we met at the mayor's house, joining in the dance or game of cards which they got up for our amusement. The morning I left Bordeaux I found that I had my old horse Knockcrockery on my hands, and not wishing to let him fall into strange hands who might maltreat him, I had him led out of the stable, and took aim at a white star he had on the forehead with my pistol. He fell dead at my feet without any apparent pang.

My general got me a passage to England in a man-of-war brig, the *Thais*, commanded by Captain Weir. We had a very pleasant party on board, amongst the rest a remarkably handsome lady, the wife of Sir Peter Parker, who had been ordered off to America, and the Captain was kindness itself. We had a roughish passage across the Bay of Biscay; we were obliged to take shelter for a night in the Scilly Islands, and the next day I had the inexpressible pleasure of landing at Falmouth, and immediately took my place in one of the stagecoaches of that day, for London.

It happened to be a Sunday: the whole of the population were turned out in their best apparel, and were all rejoicing at the termination of the war, the return of peace and plenty; and after having passed two years almost entirely deprived of female society, I was immensely struck with the great beauty of my countrywomen as we passed along the road, which certainly exceeds that of any other I had seen; and after some hours' travelling, I found myself once more in delightful London, having passed through some of the most charming counties in dear and beautiful England.

In future essays, should I survive to write, I shall state how I got my commission in the Guards, served for seven years in London, Windsor, and the Tower, and at the end exchanged on half-pay.

CHAPTER 8

Anecdotes of War

In my last chapter, which brought the Peninsular War to a glorious termination, I omitted, or rather forgot, several anecdotes which I have since recalled to memory, and should not wish to leave out of my *Recollections*, as they might be interesting to many of my gentle readers, for they have brought forth many letters which are most gratifying and complimentary to me. In the few observations which I made referring to my late brother-in-law, Stepney St. George, I forgot to mention what had happened to him at the Battle of Albuera, before my time, but related to me by himself and his brother officers. In that very bloody and almost doubtful victory he received a very severe wound, and lay upon the field of battle.

A Polish lancer, probably attracted by his bright scarlet coat and gold epaulets (for he, having plenty of private means, was always well dressed), gave him a poke with his lance, and finding there was life in him, thought he should perhaps secure an officer of high rank. He took him by the collar, and was dragging him into the French lines in a state of insensibility, when St. George was aroused from his swoon by something warm trickling down upon his head. It proved to be the life-blood of the Pole, who had received a mortal wound from a musketshot, which relieved him of his burden, and poor St. George managed to crawl back into the British lines, and was saved.

Within the last four days previous to the time I now write (the 10th of June, 1873), I was down in the County Roscommon, and went to have a day's fishing in the Carnadoe Waters, a tributary to the Shannon. On the shore, where our boats awaited us, there was a small farmhouse, which I heard was occupied by a very old man who had been in the Peninsula. I do not like missing an opportunity, now very rare, of meeting with one of these old veterans, and went in. I found

The escape of Stepney St. George
at the Battle of Albuera.

a remarkably fine specimen of an old soldier, a man of the name of Washington, in his ninety-seventh year, as straight as a ramrod, with all his faculties, sight, hearing, and memory perfect; but what was my surprise when I found he had been one of my old Light Infantry Company in the 31st Regiment? He had been out with the regiment since the commencement of the war in the year 1808, and in all the general actions of that exciting and interesting period, without a wound up to the 13th of December, 1813.

He was as much surprised as I was, and could scarcely believe I was the youth who commanded the company the day he was wounded. He stripped his leg and showed me where the ball had passed through his knee; he told me that I said to him, "Washington, you are down at last," and that he replied, "I shall soon be up again." He went to the rear on my horse, and met Lord Wellington and Sir R. Hill, who desired him to keep on the low ground, or he and the horse would be knocked to smash in a few moments, the shot and shell were falling so fast.

He got to the rear, and was sent to the military hospital at Cambo, and proceeded from thence by St. Jean de Luz to England, where he recovered from his wound, served for ten years more in the first battalion in Sicily, Naples, &c., and then retired on a pension of 1s. *per diem*. I hope I shall be able to get this small pension increased to 2s. 6d. for the remainder of this poor old man's life, and will be quite ready to certify what I know of his former military career.

When he took me by the hand, after recalling many of the scenes we had passed through, and the name of almost every officer that we both so well remembered, the poor old man shed tears, and I could scarcely refrain from responding to them. He mentioned the three colonels I have already alluded to in a former chapter, and named the colonel who, having been shot through the trousers, went to the rear, and, instead of the doctor, one of the regimental tailors was sent to dress his wound.

I have also received a most interesting letter from another gentleman whom I had formerly mentioned, and it is so creditable to him, so gratifying and flattering to me, that I asked his permission to bring it into this chapter, and the following is a copy of it. I have accepted his kind invitation to visit him in Norfolk, and look forward to introduce my daughters, who are also invited, to his family with feelings of great pleasure:

THE MEETING OF THE VETERANS

Wroxham House, Norwich,
May 12th, 1873.

My Dear Sir,—A friend of mine, who reads with great interest your *Scraps from Recollection,* has pointed out to me your complimentary mention of my name in the April number of the *St. James' Monthly Review*. I have a pleasing recollection of my short acquaintance with you at Vieux Mouguerre, where the light company of the 31st joined the Buffs, 57th and 66th Light companies of Sir John Byng's brigade, and have ever entertained a lively and grateful remembrance of your kindness and good offices in hastening to my assistance when I fell, severely wounded in both legs, on the afternoon of the 13th of December, 1813. You then very considerately bound up the extensive wounds in my left leg with a sash, making with a piece of stick a temporary tourniquet, thus saving me probably from bleeding to death during my long and painful carriage to the rear. I remember, too, that you exerted your authority to compel some French prisoners we had captured to assist a few of our own slightly wounded men to carry me off.

On my way I met the Duke of Wellington and his staff riding to the front. He, commiserating my shattered condition, stopped to ask my name, &c., and sent an *aide-de-camp* to fetch a surgeon, pointing out some huts to which I might be carried. I, however, (I had many years after an opportunity of thanking him,) finding that shells from the enemy were falling near the huts, went on to Mouguerre, and had the satisfaction of meeting the surgeon of the Buffs coming out under Lord Wellington's orders, *viz*. Dr. Sheckleton, afterwards an eminent *accoucheur* in Dublin, where I visited him about forty years ago. When the army crossed the Adour, in the early spring, I was removed to St. Jean de Luz, and about June embarked for England in 1814. By the blessing of God and a strong constitution I had quite recovered by the summer of 1815, and was walking on an artificial leg, riding on horseback, and not long afterwards following the hounds. Placed on the G.R.V. Battalion, I was allowed to retire on full pay for life as a lieutenant of seven years' standing and with a captain's pension.

In 1838 I married a sister of Sir Robert John Harvey, K.C.B., whom you may remember on the quartermaster general's staff, and have seven children living; my eldest son is a barrister; my second son, a lieutenant in the 8th Regiment King's, has just now an appointment to survey, with other officers, 'Cannock Chase,' in Staffordshire, with a view to autumn manoeuvres there.

In 1847, an old friend of mine left me a charming residence here, with good estates connected, and I then took the name of Humphrey in addition to that of Blake (at his request); and by the death of my elder brothers I have since succeeded to a family property, also in this neighbourhood. I am now seventy-seven years and a half old, am a J.P. and D.L., county of Norfolk, and still enjoy good general health. I should be well pleased to have you for a guest at Wroxham, if you would be tempted into this country to see Hunstanton Hall, the ancient seat of the L'Estranges, about which you used to inquire of me, believing your Irish branch to be descended from the Norfolk family. I have some photographs of the hall made many years ago from my drawings, but you had better see the place itself, which is very interesting, I assure you. Sincerely yours,

E. Blake Humphrey.

After this digression I return to London, where I had just arrived at the conclusion of my last chapter. The allied armies had entered and taken possession of Paris. Prussia, groaning under the barbarous treatment they had received from the French Army when in occupation of their beloved Fatherland, was panting for revenge, and it required all the energy of our great duke to prevent their committing the greatest atrocities. They were determined to demolish the Bridge of Jena and the column in the Place Vendôme; and the duke, it was said, found great difficulty in persuading old Blucher to exert his influence with his noble army and prevent their retaliating on the inhabitants of Paris the many acts of oppression which the French Army had committed on most of the families or friends of the Prussian soldiers. Order, however, was at length restored, and the allied sovereigns, with Wellington and Blucher, arrived in London. They were of course received with acclamation, and London was *en fête* for a considerable time.

It was resolved that they should go in procession and great pomp to St. Paul's; I suppose, to return thanks for the great event that had restored peace to Europe after these long and sanguinary wars. All London of course turned out to see this great procession, and it was with difficulty and considerable cost that a window or a seat or even stand-

Hunstanton Hall Co of Norfolk

ing-ground could be obtained. I, with my cousin Edmund, who had also arrived in town, was so fortunate as to get an order for Northumberland House, and accordingly proceeding to the roof of that noble building, we took up our position just under the straight tail of the lion that crowns the edifice; from thence we had a splendid view of the procession as it passed under us up the Strand, and we recognised many of the gallant heroes whom we recollected to have seen during that part of the Peninsular War in which we had taken a part.

After a short stay in London I began to feel a strong wish to return and visit my family in Ireland, to whom I was devotedly attached, and soon took a place in the Holyhead mail, for there was no steam in those days, *en route* for Dublin. When I arrived there I found that most of my family were in the county of Sligo, at Temple House, the residence of Colonel Perceval, who had been married to my eldest sister before I went out to the Peninsula, and I found a letter from her to inform me that a coach had lately been placed on the road that actually performed the journey in a single day.

I lost no time in Dublin, and after a journey that I thought would never come to an end, found myself drawing up to the hall-door of one of the oldest inhabited thatched houses in Ireland. I thought I saw a perfect angel at the door, and in a minute was in the arms of my favourite sister Sophie, two years younger than myself, whom I had left what is called a slip of a girl, but now developed into the most lovely and magnificent woman that I thought I had ever laid my eyes on. I need not describe the reception I met with from every member of the family as well as herself. She afterwards became the wife of E. J. Cooper, Esq., of Marknee Castle, for many years member of Parliament for the county of Sligo.

But little more than a year after her marriage, in her confinement of her firstborn son, they were both carried from Dublin to a vault in the church of Collooney, where her husband erected to her memory a very beautiful monument, which was sculptured in Italy. I had the melancholy happiness, in company with my cousin, who afterwards became my most beloved wife, of receiving her last sigh. In consequence of the youth of both parties, their union was protracted for upwards of a year, and in my opinion should be a warning to all parents not to permit their daughters to have long engagements before marriage, as it is to this I attribute her premature death.

After my arrival at Temple House, where I need not say I enjoyed the greatest happiness for some time, I made a tour of visits to all my friends, and was received with acclamation wherever I went, after the dangers I had escaped. I kept a sharp lookout for all the *Gazettes*, in expectation of seeing my name as an officer in the Guards, according to my general's (now Sir John Byng) kind promise.

A vacancy did not occur till after the Battle of Waterloo, when to my great joy, at the head of five death-vacancies in that sanguinary action, I saw that I was gazetted an ensign and lieutenant in the 3rd Foot Guards. It would be presumptuous of me to attempt any detail of that great battle which has been described a hundred times; but one name in the long list of killed was that of my dear and well-beloved cousin Edmund. His leg was carried off by a cannon-ball when *aide-de-camp* to the gallant Sir Denis Pack. A successful amputation was performed; he was going on well, when a false alarm was spread by some of the fugitives, of which there were many, that the French were coming on.

With a lively recollection of his former imprisonment and escape from Verdun, he dreaded falling into their hands again, and insisted on being removed. The moving brought on haemorrhage, and he sank from loss of blood. Thus fell as noble and gallant an officer as any in His Majesty's service, deeply lamented by every member of his family, to which he was an ornament, and by the numerous friends who knew his value and his worth, and by none more than his gallant general, Sir Denis Pack, who left recorded the very high opinion he entertained of him, and which was sent to me by his heir, when Sir Denis, after many years, passed away himself. It is a great pleasure to me to dwell on the "recollections" of this young hero, as I may justly call him; and I am sure it will be grateful to many members of his family, particularly his sister, who is still living, (1874), at a very advanced age, that I have had this opportunity of recording his many amiable qualities as a soldier, a son, and a brother. Since writing the above I have found amongst my papers Sir Denis Pack's testimony, which I give from his own manuscript:—

Abbeville, December 28th, 1815.

I am informed that Mrs. L'Estrange, the mother of my late much-lamented *aide-de-camp*, Major L'Estrange, has applied for relief from the Waterloo Fund, stating in her memorial that she is the widow of an officer who sold out of the army after twenty-five years' service; that her husband afterwards served for many years and till his death as adjutant of a regiment of Militia; but having sold out of the army, as above stated, he left her without a pension and in very distressed circumstances, with a family of five sons and three daughters. The second son, a lieutenant in His Majesty's Navy, distinguished himself in several engagements, and in one had his arm carried off by a cannon-shot, and in the sequel lost his life in a line-of-battle ship on the coast of France.

Of the merits of the eldest, who fell in the Battle of Waterloo, I am really unable to speak in adequate terms. He was gallant and accomplished, and endeared to me by all the ties that can attach a general to his *aide-de-camp*. He was recommended by the Duke of Wellington for the rank he held, and I have no doubt that had he survived His Grace's last glorious victory, he would have obtained a lieutenant-colonelcy in the same honourable way. He joined the 71st Regiment when very young, served with it in Europe, Africa, and America, and shared in the well-earned fame of the corps, beloved and esteemed by all his brother officers. His mother has stated that out of his little income he allowed her one hundred a year.

I have no doubt he did, and by his generous disposition greatly contributed to the family's support, which by his fall has, in truth, suffered an irreparable loss. I have felt myself in duty called upon to offer this, believe me, gentlemen, but just tribute of praise to the memory of an officer of very great promise, who has fallen in the service of his country; and I shall only further beg leave to recommend to your warmest protection the family so much dependent on him, and which consists, as I have stated, of a widow (his mother), two daughters, and three sons, two of whom are in the army, one a lieutenant in the 24th Regiment, the other an ensign in the 71st. This statement I believe to be perfectly correct, and I shall add that I have always heard that her husband bore an excellent character as an officer and a gentleman.

  I have the honour to be, gentlemen,
    Your sincere and obedient servant,
                D. Pack.

Ireland was in a very critical state when the Battle of Waterloo was fought; disaffection to the British Government was wound up to the highest pitch. Had Wellington been defeated, there is little doubt but Ireland would have been up in arms; and so well were matters organised, that the news of the great battle was known in most parts of the country before any official account was published. There were no electric wires in those days, but it was perfectly evident, from the downcast countenances of those who were well known to be disaffected, that they had received intelligence that they did not like.

At the time the news arrived I was in Limerick, on a visit to Bishop Warburton; his son, the archdeacon, was a great friend of our family, and he had invited me down with my horse (a celebrated hunter, called "White Stockings," from having legs of that colour), to have some hunting with Mr. Tuthill's celebrated pack of stag-hounds, and to have some cock-shooting at Curragh, the seat then of Mr. Spring Rice, afterwards Lord Monteagle, and other places in that fine county. The peasantry there, as well as in my own county, the King's, were very generally of that sect who bore so much enmity to England; and you could see by their faces how chapfallen they were. I lost no time in returning to my father's house at Moystown, to be greeted as a guardsman, and could scarcely avail myself of the month's leave I was given before joining my battalion in London. This period soon passed away, and my arrival was reported at the orderly-room at the Horse Guards.

Immediately after joining I received a letter from my old general and patron, Sir John Byng, from the army of occupation at Cambray, offering me the appointment of *aide-de-camp* in place of Captain Dumerresq, who had been severely wounded at Waterloo. I instantly went to the colonel of my regiment, the late Duke of Gloucester, to ask His Royal Highness's permission to go out and join Sir John Byng as *aide-de-camp*, who had so kindly remembered me. His Royal Highness told me that there was a rule in his regiment, that no officer should go on the staff till he had done a year's duty with the regiment. I replied that I had done two campaigns in the Peninsula; but his Royal Highness, who was rather obtuse, could not see the relevancy of my argument, and I had to make my bow, rather depressed in having lost what was the great object of all young officers, an appointment on the staff.

I, however, determined to make the best of it, and began to think that a campaign or two in London was not so bad after all; and I returned to my duty and to make the acquaintance of my brother officers, who nevertheless thought I was rather hardly treated. At that time there was a splendid lot of young officers in the regiment, amongst others the celebrated Dick Armit, who became my bosom friend, and of whom I hope to have a great deal more to relate. There were several Irishmen at the time in it; next above me was the Hon. Jack Westenra, who is still alive, (1874); Chidley Coote, brother of Sir Charles, who is also still alive, (1874), and, when I saw him lately, looking as well and as cheery as ever; Lord Rokeby, then Henry Montagu; George Anson, afterwards the general who died near Lucknow; Sir David Baird, and that uncommon jolly fellow and good sportsman, Jack Standen; also the late Sir Charles Phipps, and the present Sir William Knollys; all these are well-known and almost public characters, and it can easily be guessed that with such a set of companions I scarcely regretted not being with the army of occupation at Cambray.

I soon made my way into the best society in London, and passed many happy, uncommonly gay, and very pleasant days. Nor can I omit to mention my most excellent friend Forster, now, (1874), a general officer, and for many years the well-known military secretary to His Royal Highness the Duke of Cambridge, the Royal Duke who has commanded, and, I rejoice to say, still continues, (1874), to command with so much ability and so much popularity and efficiency the army which, alas! I have taken my leave of finally, having received a valedictory letter, written by His Royal Highness's commands, from General Egerton, which I am proud of and mean to hand down as an heirloom in my family.

There are many other names, now that I have begun to mention them, I ought not to omit. Berkeley Drummond was our adjutant, afterwards succeeded by Sir Archibald Murray, who, as well as his clever, agreeable and handsome brother, Digby Murray, were great friends of mine: they were in some way related to Lord Digby's family, and as my second sister Mary had married a Digby, Richard, who resided at Geashill Castle in the King's County, it formed a sort of bond between us. He was cousin and agent to the then Lord Digby, of a peculiarly strong religious turn of mind, which many of the Digbys possess. I always felt that he was a little too good for me, but he did not survive more than a year, when he fell a victim to consumption.

My sister, to whom he left all his property, was delivered of a posthumous son, a fine boy; he lived to be three or four years old, and was carried off by croup. My sister married, secondly, the talented gentleman now, (1874), at the head of what remains of the old Irish Church; a Church which, pounded and compounded, commuted and disinherited, but not disgraced, I am fully convinced will yet arise, like the Phoenix, out of her ashes.

My sister left a large family by her second marriage, many of whom survive, (1874), and therefore I am silent. She died in Rome, and was buried in the English burial-ground there. I had heard that the authorities there refused to record on her tombstone the inscription her husband had penned; indeed I believe Chief Justice Whiteside mentions the circumstance in his book; I being at Mentone, on a visit to two of my daughters who, alas! are both gone now, determined to visit my sister's grave, and accordingly proceeded by Leghorn to Rome.

After visiting many of the wonders of that wondrous city, I went to the Vatican, and sent in my card to Monsignor Talbot, a countryman whose family were well known to me. He was, I believe, the Pope's Chamberlain—if his Holiness possesses such a feminine appendage. The *monsignor* received me very kindly.

I told him the object of my visit, that I had seen the mutilated inscription. He asked me what the words were that were omitted. I told him I believed they were, "In sure and certain hope of a blessed resurrection," and the word "Rev." preceding her husband's name. He told me that there was only one name their Church condemned without redemption. He then asked me the date; I told him, and he seemed relieved, and said that was before the present Pope had occupied the chair. I said "Yes," and observed that I did not think his present Holiness would sanction such an illiberal proceeding. I asked permission to pay my respects to his Holiness; there was no public day before I was to leave Rome for Naples; but a magnificent dragoon in the evening clattered into the courtyard of my hotel, with an enormous card inviting me for twelve o'clock the next day.

I got up my court-dress, and Ribbon and Badge of St. Patrick, and presented myself in due time, and was immediately ushered by myself into the room; his Holiness was sitting also quite alone. He received me with great urbanity, and very soon placed me at my ease, and we had a very long conversation in broken French, at which we were neither of us great adepts. He asked me where I came from, and whither I was going. He seemed much pleased to learn that I came from a country where he had so many friends, asked me who was Lord Lieutenant, and when I named the Earl of Carlisle he seemed a little put out; when I told him I was going to Corfu, he told me that only a day or two before he had ordained a bishop for that island, and recommended me to make his acquaintance, which I did, and found him everything his Holiness represented him to be. I was greatly struck by the benevolent and truly religious appearance of his Holiness; and when he stood up and held out his hand to me with the Fisherman's ring on it, I did not hesitate to kiss it; and received with the greatest humility and respect the blessing of the man whom I had so often heard disrespectfully spoken of in my own country.

Appendix

1

I have since received a most interesting *Memoir* of the late Major Edmund L'Estrange, 71st Highland Light Infantry, written by his brother Lieutenant-Colonel A. R. L'Estrange, late 71st Highland Light Infantry, whose death was announced in the "Obituary" of the *St. James's Magazine and United Empire Review*, August, 1873:

> *June 17th.*—At 17, Howard Place, Edinburgh, Lieutenant-Colonel Anthony Roger L'Estrange, retired full-pay, Her Majesty's 71st Highlanders, son of the late Captain Anthony L'Estrange, late of the 88th Connaught Rangers, and youngest brother of the late Major Edmund L'Estrange, 71st Highlanders, who was killed at Waterloo. Born in the early part of 1800, Colonel L'Estrange entered the army in 1815, and was present at the Battle of Waterloo, in the 71st Regiment, in which regiment he served until 1856, when, as major, he retired on full-pay from the army. This officer was therefore the brother of one of the two prisoners who escaped from Verdun and Bitche, the story of which was so graphically told by Sir George L'Estrange in the November number of the *St. James's Magazine* for 1872.

Colonel A. R. L'Estrange' s *Memoir* of his brother Edmund is as follows:—

> *The following Scraps are Roger's, every line;*
> *Pray, gentle reader, take them not for mine.*

The subject of this narrative obtained a commission in the 71st Regiment in 1804, at that time commanded by the noted Colonel Pack. He accompanied his regiment with the expedition to the Cape of Good Hope, served with the corps at the capture of Cape Town, and the total defeat of the enemy on that occasion. After this affair the 71st proceeded to South America, where it was actively engaged in the operations against the enemy.

The contest was at first crowned with success; but other events of an unforeseen nature, especially the disgrace of General Whitelock, commanding the forces, led to the defeat of the English, who were overpowered and made prisoners of war, Buenos Ayres falling into the hands of the enemy. According to some reports then in circulation, it was given out that the flints were removed from the fire-arms of our soldiers, but in what manner never clearly came to light. The British officers were escorted by couples into the interior of the country.

The late Major-General Macdonald, of the Royal Artillery, was Ensign L'Estrange's companion on the journey: they were conducted fifteen hundred miles from Buenos Ayres into the wildest part of South America, and detained as prisoners upwards of twelve months.

About this period Colonel Pack effected his escape from the enemy under very trying circumstances. A humorous rhyme came out at the time relating to that gallant officer's flight:—

> *The devil break the gaoler's back,*
> *That let thee loose, sweet Denis Pack.*

A treaty of peace was soon afterwards brought about, and the British troops returned to England.

In 1806 Ensign L'Estrange was promoted to a Lieutenancy in the 71st. He accompanied them with the expedition to Portugal, under the late Sir John Moore, at the breaking out of the Peninsular War; and served in the various operations of the army until the beginning of 1809, when he was again taken prisoner.

The following extract is taken from a journal of the late Sir Benjamin D'Urban:—

In the latter end of 1808, I was employed on the quartermaster-general's staff. I was sent on a service of observation of great importance to ascertain the real movements of a French corps, under Marshal Lefevre, that had arrived at Placencia and Coria, and seriously menaced the frontiers of Portugal (then very defenceless).

Major Guy L'Estrange, an old and dear friend of mine, of the 31st Regiment, and his cousin Lieutenant Edmund L'Estrange, of the 71st Regiment, at their own desire accompanied me, and we proceeded with all possible speed to Legura, Alcantara, and Coria, where we came into the immediate neighbourhood of the French corps, and were enabled to watch it closely, and send back to Portugal correct intelligence of its movements.

In the course of this service, which required great circumspection, I was deeply indebted to the active ability of my two companions, and I well remember the sagacity and spirit of enterprise of Lieutenant L'Estrange, and the great advantage besides which I derived from his knowledge of the Spanish language, of which I was then sadly ignorant. Thus we attended Sir Robert Wilson in the desultory but very enterprising operations in which he was then incessantly engaged, and which had for their object to deceive the enemy, and delay as long as possible his nearer advance to learn the defenceless condition of the frontiers of Portugal.

Very valuable and gallant were the services of Lieutenant L'Estrange in all these enterprises, until at length Sir Robert Wilson in person surprised and carried off a small post of French cavalry near Calvedella, in the attack of which Edmund L'Estrange's behaviour was as usual excellent. But the French reserve coming rapidly to the rescue with an overpowering superiority, as well in number as in quality of their force, overthrew and routed us, and pursued us very inveterately.

In the confusion of our retreat poor L' Estrange fell into the hands of the French cavalry, who surrounded and made him prisoner. He was then sent into France, and I deeply lamented his loss on every account, public and private, for he was a most amiable and estimable young man; and a more gallant and intelligent officer, or one of greater promise, it has never been my good fortune to meet with; and I had afterwards good reason to know how highly he was thought of by his regimental commanding officer, Sir Denis Pack (whose *aide-de-camp* he afterwards became), and by his whole regiment.

His sudden capture was entirely owing to the horse he rode having formerly belonged to the French cavalry.

L'Estrange was at this period employed in reconnoitring at some distance in advance of his friends, when he was unexpectedly surprised by a mounted picquet of the enemy, who, upon observing him, caused their trumpeter to blow the charge; his horse became instantly unmanageable; the well-known martial sound completely fascinated the animal, so that all his efforts to spur him on proved fruitless; from this unlucky event he was surrounded and made prisoner; the officer in command coming up at the moment in full gallop, made a cut at him with his sabre, which, however, L'Estrange dexterously parried, and he then was forced to surrender.

Lieutenant L'Estrange was now taken under escort overland to Verdun, in the east of France, a station selected by their government for English prisoners of war. The journey occupied some time, and was tedious and fatiguing. He arrived at his destination in March, 1809, and was detained for a considerable period at that place on parole.

At first he became reconciled in a measure to his position, in consequence of the hospitality evinced by the French residents at Verdun to the English prisoners.

Balls and parties succeeded each other, and a variety of amusements introduced, to all of which they were invited. At a ball *masqué* L' Estrange appeared in female costume, where the following adventure occurred to him, which unfortunately resulted in a duel, and he was severely wounded.

His partner in the dance, a naval officer of the British service, was not aware of the deception; his attentions being encouraged, a flirtation ensued, which gave no little amusement to those in the secret.

During the course of the evening the officer in question discovered the imposition; but instead of taking it in good part, his anger was aroused. An apology was freely offered, and every exertion made by friends on both sides to subdue his resentment. All their efforts were unavailing; nothing would satisfy him but a hostile meeting, which accordingly took place the next morning. L'Estrange fired in the air; his opponent's shot, passing through his right side, seriously wounded him, but he ultimately made a perfect recovery. His adversary expressed deep regret for what had happened, and was particularly kind to him during his illness: they afterwards became great friends.

This incident created no little sensation in the various circles of Verdun. The police were much censured on account of the duel, and the authorities dismissed some from office; this naturally gave rise to increased animosity towards the English. Some time after he had a disagreement with a tradesman who exacted payment of his bill over again, the receipt for which could not at first be found amongst his papers, and, refusing to wait until further search had been made, hurried to the *prefect* to lodge a complaint, glad of an opportunity to exercise his power. L'Estrange was thus unjustly thrown into prison, without even giving him the satisfaction of explaining the circumstance.

However, at this period it occurred to him that he could now, with propriety and honour, effect his escape; he was tired of a life of idleness and dissipation, and longed to resume the active duties of his profession. Full of this idea, he consulted his friends on the subject, for he had many; in fact, he was a universal favourite; they all agreed that as he was imprisoned his parole became nugatory. With these assurances, he made up his mind to escape, and succeeded in doing so, disguised as a pedlar. By this arrangement, he was enabled to carry some wearing apparel without attracting particular notice.

His knowledge of the French language (which he spoke with fluency) he found of great use, but the want of a *passeport* was a terrible drawback. To avoid the police, who were constantly on his track, often puzzled him, and he was obliged to journey on foot at night, taking refuge in the woods by day. He had provided himself with a variety of costumes, yet, with all his precautions, he had the utmost difficulty to outwit the vigilance of the gendarmerie in pursuit of him.

One adventure is worth relating, and somewhat romantic. He was so closely pressed by his tormentors, that he adopted the disguise of a female, a peasant's dress which he purchased in a village at nightfall; returning with it to a neighbouring wood, his late hiding-place, he put it on, concealing the other garments there; repairing to an *auberge* for refreshment in his new character, and while in the act of partaking it, the police suddenly made their appearance. He heard them eagerly inquiring after a fugitive English prisoner, describing to the landlord a person resembling himself in all particulars; they were actually in the same room within a few steps of him, but, quietly continuing his repast, he did not attract their observation.

In the same costume he approached a cottage in the vicinity of the village, and begged a night's lodging; his request was granted. In order to baffle the designs of the police, he resolved to remain in his present concealment; the cottagers were extremely kind, and not arousing their suspicions he passed a week with those good people, assisting them to work in the fields, it being harvest time; in this manner he made himself very useful; the family consisted of the farmer, his wife, two sons, and a daughter.

After a few days the latter discovered his deception; she promised faithfully not to betray him, and she kept her word. To get away from this perilous position without delay was not an easy matter; his inventive genius did not desert him now. Feigning sickness one morning, he proposed to take charge of the dwelling while the family were at work; during their absence he fled from the cottage, and reached his hiding-place in the wood, without attracting any notice, where he had previously left his bundle.

In the afternoon observing a party of mounted *gendarmerie* proceeding towards the village, he felt convinced they were the very same that he had been in such unpleasantly close proximity to at the *auberge*: he was afterwards confirmed in this supposition. Later in the day he saw a man advancing on horseback with a pillion; reflecting upon the wisest plan to pursue, he suddenly decided how to act, and coming out of his shady recess, asked the rider to give him a lift? His request was willingly complied with. "*Montez, Mademoiselle!*" said the equestrian, and, backing the animal, our adventurer was soon seated on the pillion.

While conversing with his unsuspecting companion, who told him as an amusing piece of information, he had just met the *gendarmerie*, and they were in search of an English prisoner who had escaped from Verdun! Prudence prompted him not to be too inquisitive, in case it might lead to more awkward consequences. He had ascertained the fact without doubt that the party referred to were retracing their steps in pursuit of the fugitive, and, like hounds at fault in the chase, were trying back to find their game.

This circumstance removed considerable uneasiness from his mind, and he now hoped to be able to continue his journey with less risk of being captured. When they had travelled about two leagues he dismounted, wishing him goodnight, with many thanks for his politeness; and directed his steps towards a plantation which was some little distance from the road, where, throwing off his woman's garb for that of his own sex, and, feeling less apprehensive than he had done for some time, he lifted up his heart in gratitude to God for thus far preserving him from falling into the hands of his enemies; then, sitting down to rest in this tranquil spot, he began considering which would be the safest character to personate on his way to Rotterdam.

The female he thought objectionable, as the police might have gained information from the cottagers, of his late proceedings, and the pedlar's was equally imprudent; so he resolved to equip himself as a sailor; but, alas! on seeking through his little stock of requisites, he did not possess the necessary additions to make his toilet complete as a jolly tar; at last he decided to try the dress of a labourer seeking harvest work; with a red wig and a patch on his eye, he was sure it would be difficult for any one to recognise him. After reposing until twilight set in, he emerged cautiously from his place of concealment, and resumed his journey onwards. Here and there he succeeded in picking up the rig-out of a sailor, which he adopted.

From this period he was particularly fortunate, and finally arrived at Rotterdam without further adventure. It was in the autumn of 1810 he entered that city, and put up at an obscure inn frequented by nautical people, with a view not only of avoiding detection, but also to be in a better position of procuring a passage to England, a most difficult matter to accomplish, as the war was then at its height between the two nations, and the gendarmerie always on the *qui-vive*.

He negotiated with a smuggler to land him on the British coast for a stipulated sum; but instead of fulfilling his agreement he betrayed him to the police, and L'Estrange was arrested and put in irons. He was detained at Rotterdam until instructions were received from the government respecting his future destination.

In the meantime very vigilant measures were observed to prevent his escape; a sentry, with loaded gun, was placed outside his prison-door day and night.

When about three weeks had elapsed, an order came for his removal to the Fortress of Bitche, under a strong escort. This most trying journey lasted upwards of six weeks; his sufferings the while were truly distressing, as the *gendarmes* treated him with the utmost cruelty the whole way, and were in the habit of tying their unfortunate victim to the tail of one of their horses, thus inhumanly dragging him along. He remonstrated against such barbarous discipline as calmly as his painful position would admit of: it proved of no avail, they compelled him to submit; at the end of each weary day, he was confined in the darkest cell they could procure in the prisons of the different towns at which they halted.

During this tedious march he was deprived of the common comforts of life; he did not exchange any part of his wearing apparel, not even his shirt, the whole way; he was reduced to a shocking state of misery, a spectacle worse than the poorest beggar. On reaching the Fortress of Bitche he was placed in a dungeon heavily ironed, forty feet underground: all hopes of liberty now seemed utterly lost. Tortured in mind as well as body, together with the hardships he had endured on his journey, immured in a damp, loathsome cell, without pure air, and scarcely a glimmer of light, covered with dirt and vermin, it is. not to be supposed he could bear much longer this weight of woe.

In words of fervent prayer he besought the Almighty to release him from his agony, and ere many days had elapsed he ceased to feel at least the bitterness of his fate, as he was soon seized with a violent fever, which, for a time, rendered him insensible to the torments so mercilessly heaped upon him by his relentless persecutors.

For weeks his life was despaired of. At length he rallied, but did not recover his strength for more than six months. During his convalescence he was often visited by a French officer stationed in the fortress, who appeared to take a lively interest in him, and owing to his kindness his condition was much improved. Through his intercession the irons were set aside, and he was removed to a better quarter, not so damp or deep underground.

The fever he was labouring under being of a very severe type he progressed but slowly, extreme debility followed; this humane young man procured him wine and more nutritious food than was usually allowed, indeed he was the means, in God's hands, of saving his life by his constant care. His friend had often charge of the guard over the prisoners.

The officer on this duty had a privilege of inviting one of the prisoners at a time, under certain restrictions, to his guard-room.

As L'Estrange gradually regained his health, whenever the already spoken of young Frenchman was employed in this service, he invariably selected him amongst the others; they thus became most intimate. Owing to his interference, the commandant granted him permission to exercise in a courtyard with the rest of his fellow-captives, which indulgence was not intended to extend to him in consequence of his escape from Verdun. This little walk every day, even in so narrow a space, was a great source of enjoyment after a close confinement of so many months; he now managed occasionally to hold converse with some of his companions during this hour of recreation.

Notwithstanding the endless precautions adhered to, sentries posted everywhere to prevent if possible any chance of escape, 'yet more and more arose the long pent-up, fondly cherished prospect of liberty: he panted for freedom, thoughts of dear absent friends, and distant loved scenes continually haunted him. An active mind when roused to dwell on the attainment of any particular object will never deem it hopeless, but on the contrary exert every energy to overcome the difficulties, let them be ever so great and perplexing. Such was his case.

At this period he was senior of his rank in the 71st, and what particularly annoyed him was the circumstance of so many of his juniors having been promoted over him, arising from the regulations of the service prohibiting officers obtaining advancement in their profession while prisoners of war.

L'Estrange's friends at home used every exertion to effect an exchange with a French prisoner of war of his own rank. The authorities at the Horse Guards forwarded this measure to the utmost, but the French Government was dilatory, so the application failed to come to anything, hence another disappointment. The only chance of getting away from his hated state of exile was in flight, and how to accomplish this undertaking was ever uppermost in his mind; he came to the conclusion it would be madness to attempt so hazardous a scheme without assistance, and for some time felt puzzled as to who would be the best person in the garrison to entrust with his secret plans.

At length he decided upon consulting the French officer, whose repeated acts of kindness led him now to hope he would not shrink from affording all the necessary aid to further his views; elated with these reflections, and earnestly seeking God's blessing on the result, he determined to await patiently the first opportunity. It was difficult to repress the eagerness he felt for the interview to come off. Fortunately, not many days elapsed ere the longed-for event took place, by his receiving an invitation from his friend to meet in the guard-room allotted for those (as before said) on this duty. His warm-hearted companion realized his fondest expectations, entering fully into his numerous projects, and promised to help him to the utmost of his power to carry them out. And, truly, all along he never forsook him, but continued his faithful ally to the end.

They could not at first come to any definite understanding on the subject, it required some mature consideration. On one occasion L'Estrange related that during the hour's exercise in the prison-yard he had now and then spoken to a spirited lad, an English midshipman, full of life and activity, who pined so sadly to get off, talking of nothing else, poor boy. Could it be possibly arranged for them to go together? He was undoubtedly an intelligent youth, and might be of use.

After various conversations, carefully weighing every obstacle in their path, they at last agreed that the least likely chance of attracting notice was to leave the fortress in the dress of a French officer, which his friend volunteered to provide him out of his own kit, and the young middy, in a suit of livery, to pass off as his servant. The clothes were to be smuggled by degrees into each of their cells. When all this was satisfactorily accomplished, and both knew the countersign, the kindly Frenchman told them they were to prepare on such an evening, at a certain hour, for he purposed when taking his rounds to leave their dungeon-doors unlocked for a few minutes, so as to give them the opportunity of slipping out, and then he intended joining them a short distance, to guide their steps within view of the entrance-gate.

It need hardly be said how anxiously they awaited the time appointed for their deliverance. At length the lock turning grated on their attentive ears, warning them both to make their exit at once, when the officer silently approached according to promise, leading the way through dismal corridors, dimly lit here and there by an oil lamp, until getting out into the night air, and after going a little further, whispered a God-speed to them and hurried farewell, motioning by a gesture the path to take, soon disappeared in a contrary direction.

Our two fugitives proceeded on, until abruptly accosted by a sentinel with the usual *Qui vive?* who then turned to address his unsophisticated companion. L'Estrange recollecting at the moment he could not speak a word of correct French, quickly exclaimed, "*C'est mon domestique*." to their intense relief the sentry added, "*C'est bon; passe, mon officier*," and unfastening the postern, quietly allowed them to depart.

The formidable ramparts of the citadel frowned menacingly in the gloom, increasing the darkness as they hastily strode along: at the termination of them, without further interruptions, they found themselves on the main road, heartily thankful for their good luck so far; and breathing more freely than they had as yet done, they were enabled to converse unreservedly, the elder impressing the young fellow with him to be sure to follow his advice regarding their movements, as so much depended on prudence and forethought.

He told him his object was to reach Verdun, a distance of thirty leagues, where he had many friends and acquaintances prisoners of war, one in particular being Sir Stephen May, to whom he had communicated his intention of effecting his escape from Bitche, requesting him, if he could possibly manage it, to render any assistance in the event of his being compelled to scale the walls of that garrison, every turn of which he knew so well during his lengthened detention there.

The greatest drawback now to contend with arose from the want of a *passeport*, which precluded them from attempting to enter the town without being arrested, or to travel in any public conveyance.

It was June, 1811, between nine and ten o'clock p.m., that these two commenced their journey on foot to Verdun; the undertaking was favoured by mild, warm weather; they calculated that their escape would not be discovered until eight o'clock the next morning, when measures would be immediately taken to follow their track. L'Estrange being the most experienced, decided upon their doing as he did before, walking all night long, and resting by day in some hiding-place, from whence they might singly emerge cautiously to purchase food at unfrequented-looking farmhouses, or small village shops.

Making the most of their time, they continued steadily to advance on their way, thinking they must have now got nearly forty miles from Bitche; feeling completely exhausted, unaccustomed to exercise as they had been for months, their feet began to swell and blister most painfully; so both resolved to take refuge in the first wood they came to, and recruit their failing strength, after which one or other should sally forth to procure something to eat, as the cravings of appetite were becoming highly unpleasant.

L'Estrange considered it advisable then to divest, himself of the French uniform for that of a peasant, a light suit of which he had put on under the military one, with a wig and bonnet blue he had stowed away in his pretended servant's pocket before starting. Discarding his false *mustachios*, he made a bundle of the things taken off, and each gladly laid down on the soft green grass, very soon falling into a deep sleep.

From this they awoke greatly refreshed. After which he went to seek some bread or anything in that way, and shortly returned with a pretty fair supply of what they were so much in need of; partaking of their frugal meal, they again set out with renewed vigour, L'Estrange carrying the bundle of clothes under his arm. It was now the dusk of the evening, and the stars were twinkling numerously in the dark blue canopy above, and thoughts of the mighty Creator of all things roused feelings of love and gratitude to God for their safety thus far.

These young men knew their capture would be certain should their pursuers overtake them: although they felt very stiff in their limbs on resuming the journey, they fully determined not to stop until Verdun came in sight, except for a short time, during the heat of the next day, so on they went the whole night. The hot morning sun became at length very overpowering. The midshipman declared his toe-nails were coming off, and sure enough on examination it was found to be the case.

Seeing a stream of cool water, in it they bathed their weary feet, and found it most soothing; they fain would have stayed on there, but it was too near the high road. About a quarter of a mile distant appeared a thick plantation: to that they directed their steps, where they managed to get several hours' needful rest. Upon arising, contrary to L'Estrange's advice, his companion said he must bathe his feet once more in the water they were at in the morning; the former told him very probably he might be perceived, and if spoken to, not knowing the language well, would undoubtedly cause suspicion; he would persist in going, as his feet were so painful the temptation could not be resisted.

L'Estrange watched his receding figure, anxiously trusting he would come back all right. But it was otherwise ordained, for hour after hour passed without his doing so; much alarmed, and heartily grieved for his friend's imprudence, a dozen times he was on the point of going in quest of him, when voices and the sound of horses' feet in the distance warned him what madness it would be to venture out. Alas! poor fellow! that he had been seized by the police there could be little doubt.

Quite unnerved and depressed by what had happened, the perils of his own position weighed more heavily on his mind now than when shared with by another. He knew his chief chance of safety was to remain perfectly still until darkness set in; he singled out the largest tree to climb into, should he hear any one approaching his place of concealment.

It was with deep feelings of sadness for the fate of his less fortunate comrade, that he started once more on his way much later than usual, thinking about sixteen miles further would bring him to the walls of Verdun, where he fully expected to meet Sir Stephen May waiting to render the assistance he had solicited from him, to get into the town. Buoyed up with this hope, he made all the speed he could; but on arriving at the wished-for haven great was his disappointment to find his friend had mistaken the point of rendezvous.

Owing to this he had to stop outside the town all night, to try and scale the walls without help was the height of folly; overcome with fatigue and hunger he continued for a long time in a sort of stupor, until daylight roused him to a deeper sense of his helpless condition; he was completely at a loss what course to pursue, if he was much longer in his present destitute state he must perish from hunger; if he surrendered, the horrors of a dungeon awaited him: in this desponding mood his attention was attracted by observing the approach of some waggons loaded with hay, proceeding towards the entrance-gate; suddenly a new means of deliverance flashed across his brain, his plan was instantly formed, of cautiously drawing near to, and walking by the side of one of them, shaded by its bulky freight from the driver's view; strange to say, in this simple manner he safely passed the barrier without arresting the notice of the officials employed to demand passports, their usual vigilance was at fault on this occasion. He quickly hurried to the residence of Sir Stephen May, who gave him a hearty welcome, although little expecting his arrival, having given up all hopes of his succeeding to elude the watchfulness of the *gendarmes*.

He related to his friend the history of all the sufferings he had gone through since their last meeting, not forgetting to tell the sad capture of the poor young midshipman the day before.

L' Estrange had now, as much as ever, to be on his guard to avoid discovery; for the French Government offered large rewards for his apprehension. Strict orders were given to search in every direction to find him. The dwelling of his host was frequently visited by the police, as well as the houses of all the English prisoners. His friend contrived an ingenious hiding-place for him, in a small recess annexed to their sitting-room; in this L'Estrange took refuge during the operation of searching, which answered admirably. These restrictions obliged him to be constantly on the alert.

Sir Stephen's servant (a most faithful creature) was let into the secret, after vowing never to betray him, and his efforts proved of great assistance.

Sir Stephen and he alone knew the singular position he was placed in; a telegraphic warning was established between them, the latter announcing by a peculiar whistle the approach of the enemy; owing to this arrangement L'Estrange had time to fly to his place of concealment. In consequence of having so constantly to be on the *qui-vive*, his stay at Verdun was considerably prolonged, being unable to leave the house except at night well disguised. One evening, while out in this way, the following incident occurred, showing what risk he ran.

Meeting an old brother officer, Captain R——, he was about to welcome him aloud, when L'Estrange, afraid of exciting observation, made a sign to prevent his doing so, and they passed each other without further recognition. Day by day getting more impatient with such bagatelle work, an idea suggested itself which might tend to divert the gendarmes from incessantly persecuting him. By means of the press, through the agency of his friend, he had an advertisement published in a Paris newspaper, notifying that:—

> The fugitive English officer, Monsieur L'Estrange, who absconded from Bitche, had arrived safely on the coast of France, and was supposed to be hidden near Calais, awaiting an opportunity to escape to England.

In the course of a few weeks, the result of this scheme became apparent, as the officials sensibly relaxed in their precautions, and eventually discontinued their unwelcome visits to Sir Stephen's dwelling.

This was a great victory gained, the wheel of fortune had certainly taken a turn in his favour, But he did not, however, abate in his measures to guard against surprise; the reward offered to secure him was too tempting a bait to be altogether lost sight of.

To obtain a *passeport* now exclusively occupied his thoughts, as being unprovided with one prevented his progress onwards.

Sir Stephen May at last helped him out of this dilemma by rather a questionable mode of transaction, but which was happily crowned with success. He happened to be at a stationer's shop, where he was in the habit of dealing; while employed in selecting some articles he required, he was accidentally shown the *passeport* forms, this was a good opportunity of realising the wishes of L'Estrange: to purchase any would only lead to suspicion, so he resolved to take possession of some of them secretly; when the shopman was otherwise engaged he cleverly managed to pocket a couple unobserved, and he returned in the highest spirits, triumphantly displaying his treasures to the astonished gaze of L'Estrange.

The next consideration was how to fill up one of these forms in the usual way, with a description of the bearer, his age and profession; it was a puzzling task to undertake, and which required much practice at dissimulation to accomplish; with an old *passeport* of his friend's he commenced copying all the signatures of the prefects, and in a short time completed it so dexterously that the closest observer could not detect the fraud. Although very fragile, the identical *passeport* is still, (1874), in existence.

Another obstacle had still to be overcome before he could leave Verdun; it was necessary to have his *passeport* examined by the authorities. To attain this object he employed Sir Stephen's trusty servant to concoct a plan for getting it done. He accordingly left the precious document at the *passeport* office with a message from the owner, saying he was unable to present it himself as his time was so fully occupied, but would call for it in a few days.

The servant then deputed an acquaintance to apply for it at the appointed hour, requesting him to state that pressure of business was the cause of *monsieur* not doing so. The paper was handed to the messenger, signed in regular form, without remark, the servant, cautious and intelligent, remained at some distance from the office, anxiously awaiting the result; after receiving it safely, he quickly hastened home to his master, highly delighted in having thus easily outwitted the officials, and exultingly delivered it to L'Estrange, who warmly thanked this worthy man for the service he had so cleverly performed.

One day following, Sir Stephen was informed, during a conversation with a French officer of the garrison, that the government had come to the conclusion the British officer who escaped from Bitche had reached Calais; although strict search was desired to be made in all directions, no tidings had since been heard of him.

Nothing in the shape of news could just then have pleased L'Estrange more; possessed as he now was of the long coveted *passeport*, he decided at once upon leaving Verdun, dressed again in the French uniform which he wore with such success on his departure from Bitche; assuming a black wig and mustachios of the same dark hue, he presented a most imposing appearance, feigning the name of Captain Robert, journeying to the seat of war in Spain, to rejoin his regiment. Before starting, he found it absolutely necessary to replenish his scanty wardrobe, which consisted only, when he arrived in his humble garb at Verdun, of the small bundle already twice mentioned, containing the uniform he was then wearing.

Having completed all these arrangements to his satisfaction, and feeling most thankful to God for his present brighter prospects, after bidding a long farewell to his good and kind friend, not forgetting the faithful attendant whose efforts had been so useful, he left Verdun by the night diligence in the middle of April, 1812, and reached Paris without any particular occurrence, his *passeport visé* by authority gave him assurance and safety; passing through fortified towns it was examined but not very closely, seeing that the owner was a military man.

His place of abode in the French capital was a quiet hotel in a remote quarter of the city, where he changed his uniform, and put on civilian's clothes, thinking he would be less remarkable in them, and having more freedom of action, be the better enabled to visit and enjoy the numerous attractions in that charming metropolis. He saw the young King of Rome, son and heir of the great Napoleon (whose sad fate was little contemplated then). Having satisfied his curiosity with all that was to be seen in the chief city of France, his next care was to prepare for his journey onwards, and to get his *passeport* once more *visé* without creating suspicion, which he was fortunate enough to get done without much delay. So he started again by the diligence for Bordeaux, disguised similarly as on leaving Verdun.

The only event which took place in going there worth mentioning, happened during a conversation with two fellow-travellers, French officers; one of them asked him if he was a Frenchman, to which he replied he was a Dutchman, but had been long resident in France. He told them this as he thought the language of that country the most unlikely for his companions to understand. This opinion proved correct, for they pressed him no further, but it was a great relief to him when they happily took their departure from the diligence before it arrived at Bordeaux.

Having safely got there, he repaired to the residence of a family to whom Sir Stephen May had given him a letter of introduction, where he was most kindly received. The family promised to assist him to the utmost of their power to facilitate his escape to England. They appeared to take a warm interest in his welfare, congratulated him on his clever flight from Bitche, and assured him the authorities had abandoned the idea of recapturing him as hopeless, having come to the conclusion that he had already reached England. This was all very satisfactory; he felt quite at home with these hospitable people, and began at once consulting them regarding the most prudent plan of regaining his native land. He left off the uniform, appearing again as a civilian, and requested his new friends as a favour to intimate to the servants of the house that *monsieur* was a connexion of the family; a suggestion they adopted without delay, both to promote their own safety, as well as to satisfy the curiosity of the establishment.

His chief employment now consisted in making the requisite preparations for his much desired journey home. To secure a passage from Bordeaux to England, at a period when war was at its height between the two countries, was extremely hazardous and almost impossible; therefore the scheme he formed to carry out this object was a bold expedient, but none other appeared practicable, namely, to purchase a boat and sail direct for Great Britain.

In accordance with this resolution, he bought a fishing-boat, hired a servant, procured a *passeport* to proceed down the river, in which both were described as fishermen. The next thing was to lay in a supply of provisions and water; to get a chart of the river, a compass, together with nets and other fishing apparatus; having had some experience formerly in yachting, satisfied also that the sailor was well skilled, likewise that their united efforts were found sufficient to manage the small craft. In two days they got to the mouth of the river very quietly, but shortly began to feel the effects of the swell that at all times more or less agitates the Bay of Biscay.

It told at once on the frail bark they were in; one great roll of the mighty element would have quickly sent them to perdition. Up to this moment his sailor servant had no idea of the enterprise he was about to attempt; the open sea before them, a stiff breeze and the mountain-like waves of the ocean, raised him to a terrible state of alarm; he asked in a most excited manner if *monsieur* intended running out to sea. L'Estrange giving him no answer, he was on the point of raising a signal to attract the guard-ship anchored at the entrance of the harbour. L'Estrange, fully alive to the fact that his fate was sealed if the crew of the frigate took the alarm, the occasion required no wavering of purpose—at the impulse of the moment he clapped a pistol to the fellow's head and threatened to shoot him if he dared to move or utter a sound.

This had the desired effect; he remained silent and motionless for a considerable time afterwards. The wind being off the land was so far favourable for their progress, when just at this critical point, two *chasse-marées* were despatched in pursuit of them. With a fervent prayer to the Almighty to preserve him, L'Estrange put on all the sail the little smack could bear, seized the tiller from his trembling companion and struck out right from shore. They had a good offing and a good start, being separated by several miles from the enemy's boats when the chase began. They continued firing every now and then, the shots fortunately only whistling harmlessly in the air. Providentially the wind lulled, and a dead calm set in.

His servant by this time becoming more reconciled to his position, thinking it probably wisest to make the best of a bad bargain, took to the oars, and they both pulled lustily as for their lives. It was nearly dusk ere they lost sight of the persevering *chasse-marées*. All night they continued in this way, now rowing, now resting to recruit their weary frames. But towards morning the wind freshening, L'Estrange shaped his course by compass for the Basque Roads, where he knew the British fleet was at anchor on the look out for the enemy. Thus the day passed anxiously on.

However, about noon, his fondest hopes were realized by coming in sight of the English squadron. With fervent thanks to God for His great mercies and boundless joy he bore direct for them. As he approached the fleet, a boat was despatched from the flagship, with orders to board and search the stranger. During this process, L'Estrange lost but little time in apprising the crew that he was an English officer, who had escaped from France, where he had been more than three years a prisoner. Upon hearing this the honest sailors welcomed him with loud and hearty cheers.

In this rapturous manner he was conducted to the flag-ship, amidst the roars of the gallant tars. When he came to the quarter-deck the cheers and hurrahs were repeated by all the officers and seamen on board each vessel. He was then presented to the admiral, who received him with the utmost kindness, had a cabin prepared for his accommodation, providing him with every comfort. He related the outlines of his adventures to the admiral, who listened to his story with profound attention, after which he highly complimented him on his ability and tact in making such a remarkable escape.

It would be difficult to describe his feelings of happiness in finding himself at last safely on board a British man-of-war. After all the hardships and difficulties he had gone through, it graciously pleased the Almighty to crown his efforts in the end with success. Before many days elapsed, he was landed at Plymouth, where the major and corporation of that borough gave him a public dinner, on which occasion his health was drunk with all the honours.

He proceeded from Plymouth forthwith to London, and obtained an interview with his late Royal Highness the Duke of York, who gave him a most gratifying reception.

A company being then vacant in the 71st, His Royal Highness was pleased to grant his promotion; and, in addition, bestowed upon him all his back rank in the regiment as a particular mark of his favour.

He subsequently sailed for Portugal, and became *aide-de-camp* to Sir Denis Pack, then in command of a brigade of the army under Wellington. He served on his staff with that brigade, which bore a very distinguished part, to the close of the Peninsular War in 1814 He was wounded at the Battle of Vittoria, and had two horses shot under him at Toulouse, the last desperate engagement in the Peninsular War.

When at Bordeaux again, he had the pleasure of meeting the kind family, who were instrumental in assisting him in his departure from that place: they still continued to pay him every attention and hospitality.

Bonaparte having been once more proclaimed Emperor of France, after his flight from Elba in 1815, hostilities recommenced between England and France.

At the memorable Battle of Waterloo, Sir Denis Pack was a second time in command of a brigade. L'Estrange, now brevet-major, was again appointed his *aide-de-camp*.

******

Many years after this sad event, Lady Pack, on the death of her husband, while looking over his private papers in a cabinet, discovered the miniature, in a red morocco case, of the subject of this short *Memoir*. She forwarded it to his youngest brother, at that time captain in the 71st Highland Light Infantry, according to Sir Denis' desire that it should be sent to him at his death.

******

In the midst of the thickest of the carnage which took place on that ever to be remembered day, this gallant young fellow was amongst the number of those ruthlessly struck down in that terrible but victorious battle. A round-shot struck and shattered his right leg, killing his horse at the same moment. He underwent amputation of the limb, but the fearful shock to the nervous system, and excessive loss of blood, proved too much for his constitution, and he died from exhaustion. Thus fell prematurely as brave an officer as ever served in the British army, at the early age of twenty-seven, and eleven years' service, most deeply lamented by a widowed mother, and a numerous circle of sorrowing relatives and friends.

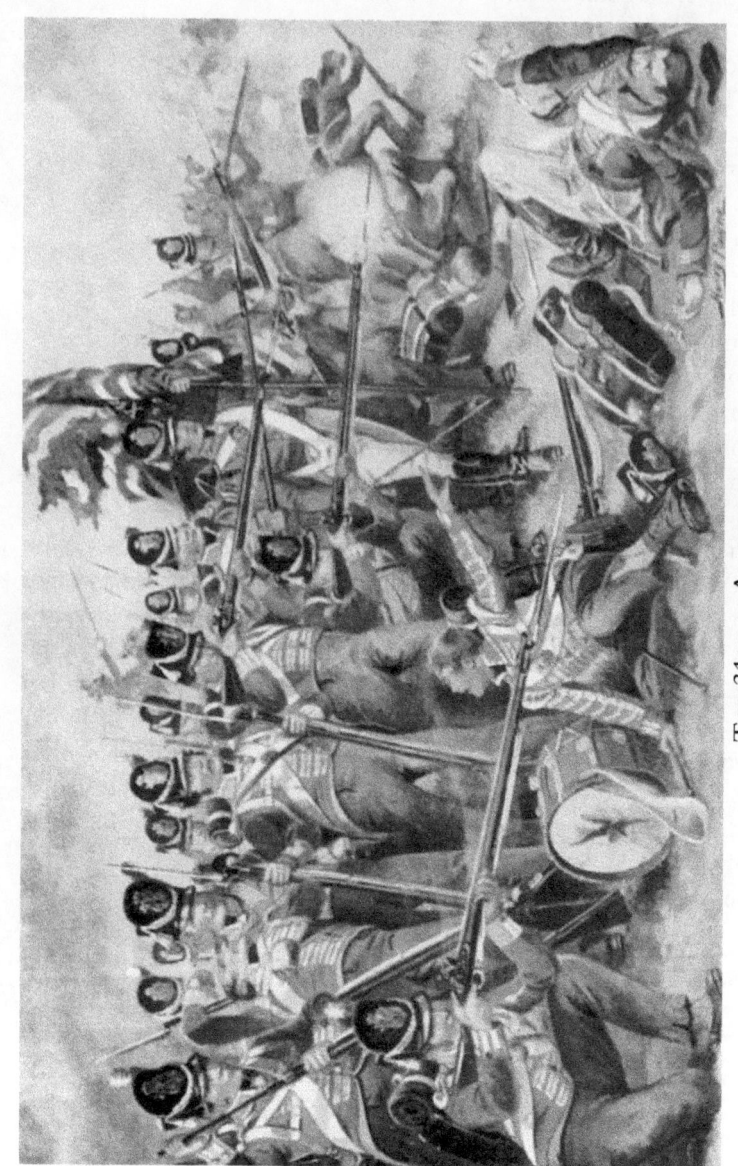

The 31st at Albuhera

The 31st or Huntingdonshire Regiment of Foot During the Napoleonic Period

Richard Cannon

First Battalion

On the 17th of October, 1797, the definitive treaty of peace between Austria and the French republic was signed at Campo Formio, so that Great Britain was left to continue the contest single-handed with France and her allies.

The threat of invasion, renewed by France, 1798, called forth the patriotic feelings of the British nation; the militia force was increased, and volunteer corps were formed in every part of the kingdom.

Napoleon Bonaparte, against whose legions in the Peninsula, in subsequent years, the Thirty-First regiment acquired great renown, was now rising step by step to that Imperial sway which he afterwards attained. The French Directory, jealous of his ambition, sent him on the expedition to Egypt, with the view of acting from that country against the British empire in India. Napoleon took Alexandria by storm, and soon established himself at Cairo. The Sublime Porte, incensed by the invasion of Egypt, declared war against France, and formed an alliance with Russia.

The fleet, which had conveyed the expedition to Egypt, was almost destroyed by Admiral Nelson in Aboukir Bay on the 1st of August. So large a portion of the French army being thus secluded in a distant land, gave fresh impulse to the Allies, and in November the island of Minorca surrendered to the British arms. In December the co-operation of Russia against France was secured by Great Britain.

At this period of the war the soldiers of the English militia regiments were permitted to extend their services to the regular army;—the Thirty-First regiment received eight hundred and fifty-three volunteers from the militia.

In March, 1799, war was declared by the French Directory against Austria, and the combined Austrian and Russian armies were so successful as to recover the greater portion of Italy.

In August, 1799, a corresponding attempt was made by Great Britain to recover Holland from the dominion of Franco, and a numerous army was selected to proceed to that country, under His Royal Highness the Duke of York, Previously to the arrival of the Duke of York, the army was commanded by Lieut.-General Sir Ralph Abercromby, K.B., with the local rank of General.

The Thirty-First regiment marched to Deal, embarked for Holland on the 8th of September, and arrived at the Holder on the 15th of the same month. The Thirty-First and other regiments were embarked after the departure of General Sir Ralph Abercromby, in order to reinforce his army. The Duke of York, having preceded these additional troops by two days, was already in command of the army, which was entrenched in the advance of the Helder on the Zuype, in which lines Sir Ralph Abercromby had, on the 10th of September, near the village of Crabbendam, repulsed the attack of the French and Dutch under General Brune.

Immediately on landing, the Thirty-First marched to the lines, and joined Major-General the Earl of Chatham's brigade, in the division of General Sir Ralph Abercromby, on the 15th of September. The Duke of York, having been reinforced by the expected arrival of a corps of twelve thousand Russians, under Lieut.-General Hermann, resolved on attacking the French position in advance of Alkmaar, reaching from Zuyder-Zee on the right, to Camperdown on the left, and embracing the town of Bergen.

The attack was made on the 19th of September, in four columns: the right, formed entirely of Russians, under Lieut.-General Hermann, moved on Bergen; the centre divisions, under Lieut.-General Dundas and Lieut.-General Sir James Pulteney, forced the village and post of Oude Carspel, on the road to Alkmaar; while the left column, in which was the Thirty-First regiment, under General Sir Ralph Abercromby, advanced to the capture of Hoorne.

The point of attack selected for Sir Ralph Abercromby's division being at a considerable distance beyond the extent of the line, the Thirty-First, and other regiments, marched at eight o'clock on the night of the 18th of September, and the movement was performed with such skill and secrecy, that Hoorne was surprised and carried on the following morning without loss, which placed the French position in considerable peril. The Russians having failed in holding Bergen, after having entered it in gallant style, rendered it impossible for the centre division to continue in possession of the posts it had acquired.

The British troops were therefore withdrawn to their former lines upon the Zuype, to which the Russians had retreated. Hoorne was evacuated, and the Thirty-First, with the other regiments of Sir Ralph Abercromby's division, returned on the night of the 19th of September to the ground they had quitted on the former evening.

From the 20th of September until the 1st of October, both armies remained within their entrenchments, strengthening their lines of defence; the French had received reinforcements, and had inundated a large tract of country on their right by cutting the sluices, thus contracting the ground of operations to six or seven miles.

The Duke of York, on the 2nd of October, made another attack on the French position between Bergen and Egmont-op-Zee. The combined attacks were made in four columns; the division under General Sir Ralph Abercromby, being on the right, marched along the beach. The left of the French Army was posted and concentrated about Bergen, a large village surrounded by extensive woods, through which passed the great road leading to Haarlem; between which and the sea was an extensive region of high sand-hills impassable for artillery. Behind the sand-hills, and to the enemy's right, through the whole extent of North Holland, lies a wet and low country, intersected with dykes, canals, and ditches. The French centre was supported by the town of Alkmaar. The battle soon became serious in front of Bergen, upon which Lieut.-General Dundas had been ordered to proceed.

Meanwhile Sir Ralph Abercromby had passed Bergen in order to turn the position of the French at Alkmaar, and overcame every opposition until he reached Egmont-op-Zee, which post was occupied in great numbers, and gallantly defended. Sir Ralph Abercromby, however, here overthrew a corps of the French Army, and wheeling his division to the left, turned the enemy's position at Bergen, upon which General Brune, the commander-in-chief of the French and Batavian Army, fell back, taking up an equally strong position at a short distance to the rear.

The Thirty-First regiment had an opportunity of distinguishing itself particularly throughout this arduous contest, which lasted from six in the morning until the same hour in the evening. In the attack of Bergen, the regiment took two pieces of artillery from the enemy; the corps on the right frequently charged with the bayonet, and lost a great number of men. The Thirty-First regiment had one sergeant and twenty-seven rank and file killed; Captain Smith, Ensign King, and fifty-five rank and file wounded.

During the night of the 2nd of October, Bergen and Egmont-op-Zee were evacuated by the enemy.

The army remained during the night on the ground it held at the close of the battle, and on the 3rd of October Alkmaar was occupied by detachments of British troops. On the 6th of October, the advanced posts in front of Alkmaar, Egmont-op-Hooff, and Egmont-op-Zee, were pushed forward, preparatory to a general forward movement. At first little opposition was shown, and the British took possession of some villages, and of a position on the sand-hills near Wyck-op-Zee; but the column of Russian troops, under the command of Major-General D'Essen, in endeavouring to gain a height in front of their intended advanced post at Baccum, was vigorously opposed, and afterwards attacked by a strong body of the enemy.

This movement obliged General Sir Ralph Abercromby to move up in support with the reserve of his corps; the French advanced their whole force; the action became general along the whole line from Limmen to the sea, and was maintained with great obstinacy on both sides until night, when the enemy retired, leaving the British masters of the field of battle. The Thirty-First regiment, on the 6th of October, had Lieutenant Forster, one sergeant, and thirty-five rank and file killed; Captain Pickering, Lieutenants Mullins, Walker, Ball, Ensigns Williams and Johnson, three sergeants, and eighty-four rank and file wounded.

In the meantime the French Army had been reinforced; the state of the weather, the ruined condition of the roads, the total want of the necessary supplies, offered great obstacles; besides which, the efforts which had been made for the liberation of Holland were not seconded by the Dutch people, so that it was determined to withdraw the British Army. A convention was ultimately concluded with General Brune at Alkmaar, on the 18th of October.

On the 16th of November the Thirty-First regiment embarked at the Texel, and landed at Deal three days afterwards, when it marched immediately to Canterbury, where the effects of the Dutch campaign began to be perceptible. Before the army left Holland dysentery had broken out among the men, arising from their exposure to the damp and fogs natural to the country, The Thirty-First lost a great number of men, from this cause, while stationed at Canterbury.

On the 15th of May, 1800, the Thirty-First regiment embarked at Dover for Ireland, landed at Cove on the 6th of June, and marched directly to Cork, where a force was collecting for a secret service, to which it was added. On the 27th of June the embarkation took place, and on the 8th of July the armament reached the Bay of Quiberon; the Twenty-Third, Thirty-First, Fifty-Second, and Sixty-Third regiments landed on the Isle de Houat, where they remained encamped, under the command of Brigadier-General the Honourable Thomas Maitland, until the 19th of August, when they again embarked and joined the expedition under Lieut.-General Sir James Pulteney, destined for the coast of Spain.

A landing was effected at Ferrol on the 25th of August; the troops advanced to the heights which overlook the town, and the Thirty-First had some skirmishing with the enemy's piquets. After viewing the town and its defences. Sir James Pulteney abandoned the idea of attacking the place; the troops were re-embarked on the following morning, and the fleet sailed for Vigo, where it arrived on the 27th of August.

Here General Sir Ralph Abercromby joined with other troops, and assumed the command of the whole force. After remaining in Vigo Bay for some time, the fleet sailed for Cadiz, where it arrived on the 3rd of October. Sir Ralph Abercromby summoned the Governor to surrender, but an epidemic fever was raging in the city, and the fleet quitted the coast for fear of infection, and proceeded to Gibraltar.

At this period General Sir Ralph Abercromby received orders from the British Government to proceed to Egypt; but the three battalions of the Ninth Foot, the second battalion of the Twenty-Seventh, the Thirty-First, and two battalions of the Fifty-Second regiment, being composed principally of volunteers from the militia, whose conditions of enlistment limited their services to time and place, were not available for the expedition to Egypt: they were accordingly ordered to proceed to Lisbon, where they arrived on the 27th of November, having suffered much from confinement on board ship, and the use of salt provisions.

On the 27th of January, 1801, the Thirty-First was again at sea, and on the 14th of February disembarked at Minorca, which had surrendered to Great Britain in November, 1798; this island was restored to

Spain at the Peace of 1802.

The successes of the British arms in Egypt, by which the French were expelled from that country, were followed by a Treaty of Peace, which was signed on the 27th of March, 1802, at Amiens, between the French Republic, Spain, and the Batavian Republic, on the one part, and Great Britain on the other. The principal features of the treaty were, that Great Britain restored all her conquests during the war, excepting Trinidad and Ceylon, which were ceded to her, the former by Spain, and the latter by the Batavian Republic. Portugal was maintained in its integrity, excepting that some of its possessions in Guiana were ceded to France. The territories of the Ottoman Porte were likewise maintained in their integrity. The Ionian Republic was recognised, and Malta was to be restored to the Knights of St. John of Jerusalem. The French agreed to evacuate the Neapolitan and Roman states, and Great Britain all the ports that she held in the Adriatic and the Mediterranean.

In May, 1802, the Thirty-First regiment sailed from Minorca for England, and early in June landed at Portsmouth, on the 19th of which month it was reduced to the Peace Establishment. In the year 1803 the regiment was removed to Jersey.

★★★★★★

While stationed at Jersey, a soldier of the Thirty-First regiment displayed the following example of courage and presence of mind:—On the 4th of June, 1804, a salute had been fired in honour of the anniversary of the birthday of King George III. The bombardier, whose duty it was to deposit the slow match in the magazine on the Town Hill at St. Heliers, after the performance of the ceremony, neglected to observe whether it was extinguished; it unfortunately was still alight, and set fire to the building; there were within the place three hundred and twenty-five barrels of powder, and, from its central situation, an explosion would have destroyed the greater portion of the town. Private William Pentenny, of the Thirty-First regiment, assisted by two inhabitants of Jersey, broke open the magazine, when another moment's delay would probably have been too late, the fire having nearly reached the spot where the powder was deposited, when he entered.

With infinite coolness and decision, he carried the nearest barrels away in his arms, and continued so to act until the whole stock was removed out of danger. This important service was highly appreciated. The Patriotic Fund at Lloyd's awarded Private William Pentenny a pension of 20*l*. a year, while the states of Jersey conferred an additional 12*l*. upon this deserving soldier, and presented to him a gold medal, struck on purpose to commemorate the achievement, which he was permitted to wear. The governor, Major-General the Honourable William Stewart, ordered a ring of silver lace to be worn round his arm as a further distinction.

✶✶✶✶✶✶

Napoleon Bonaparte was now approaching the zenith of his power: the unsettled state of affairs in France had induced him to quit his army in Egypt, and on his return the Directory was abolished, Bonaparte being appointed First Consul of the French Republic. This occurred in 1799, and in the following year Europe was astounded by his daring passage of the Alps, followed by the victory of Marengo, which caused Austria to sue for peace.

The French being driven from Egypt in 1801 by the gallant Abercromby and his brave troops, in which the Thirty-First regiment would probably have shared, had it not been for the circumstances stated, the Peace of Amiens was concluded; it, however, gave but a slight interval of tranquillity to Europe. The military spirit of the French nation had been aroused by the genius of Napoleon, who endeavoured to realise his schemes for the aggrandisement of France;— and England appeared as a barrier to his designs.

In May, 1803, the war was renewed; Hanover was overrun by the French, and severed for a time from the British Crown. An immense flotilla was also assembled at Boulogne for the invasion of England. The threat of invasion aroused the patriotism of the British people, and the most strenuous measures were pursued to defeat the French ruler's designs; the "Army of Reserve Act" was passed in June, 1803, for raising men for home service by ballot; numerous volunteer and yeomanry corps were formed in every part of the kingdom; and all party differences merged into one universal effort for the preservation of Great Britain.

On the 18th of May, 1804, Napoleon was invested with the dignity of Emperor of the French, and on the; 26th of May of the following year he was crowned King of Italy at Milan.

Further measures of defence were adopted by Great Britain, and the "Additional Force Act" was passed on the 14th of July, 1804, by which a second battalion was added to the Thirty-First regiment, to be formed of men raised in the county of Chester, for limited service.

The regiment embarked at Jersey for England on the 9th of November, and on the 27th of that month arrived at Portsmouth, whence it marched to Winchester, and received a further number of volunteers from the Militia.

On the 12th of December the Court of Spain issued a declaration of war against England, in consequence of the capture of some frigates off Cadiz, which had been intercepted while on their way to France with cargoes of treasure,—Spain having agreed to furnish a powerful aid to Napoleon.

By July, 1805, the second battalion was fully embodied, and in October proceeded from Chester to Winchester, where the first battalion was stationed.

While the French wore pursuing their victorious career in Germany, they experienced dreadful reverses from the navy of Great Britain. On the 21st of October the combined fleets of France and Spain were completely defeated off Cape Trafalgar. The victory was, however, clouded by the death of Admiral Viscount Nelson, to whose memory the highest honours were paid by a grateful and admiring nation.

On the 9th of January, 1806, the Thirty-First regiment was present at the funeral of Admiral Viscount Nelson, and formed part of the line between which the procession passed on its way to St. Paul's Cathedral, in which the admiral's remains were interred, and where a monument was erected by order of Parliament.

In November of the preceding year a squadron of English and Russian vessels landed some troops at Naples without any opposition from the Neapolitan Court. The French Emperor, on receiving intelligence of this transaction, issued a proclamation that "the Neapolitan dynasty had ceased to reign," and an army, under his brother, Joseph Bonaparte, assisted by Marshal Massena, marched for Naples. On the 15th of February the French entered that capital, and soon obtained possession of the whole kingdom, excepting Gaeta; Ferdinand IV. and his Court having previously retired to Sicily. A decree was shortly issued by Napoleon, conferring the crown of Naples on his brother Joseph, who was proclaimed King on the 30th of May.

England being desirous of preserving Sicily from the dominion of France, troops were embarked for that island;—on the 26th of April the first battalion of the Thirty-First regiment embarked at Tilbury-fort, and landed at Messina on the 26th of July.

Previously to the arrival of the Thirty-First regiment, the French had assembled a force in Calabria for the invasion of Sicily, and Major-General Stuart, commanding the British troops in that island, formed the design of cutting off the French division under General Regnier; the result was the Battle of Maida, where a victory was gained by the British troops on the 4th of July. Major-General Stuart being sensible that he could not, with his small force, maintain himself in Calabria, recrossed the straits of Messina and returned to Sicily. For this victory Major-General John Stuart received the dignity of Knight of the Bath, the thanks of Parliament, and was created Count of Maida by the King of the Two Sicilies.

Admiral Sir John Duckworth having failed in his coercive mission to detach Turkey from the interests of France, Great Britain determined to seize upon Egypt, as a check to any fresh demonstration by the French against the British possessions in the East Indies.

An armament accordingly sailed from Melazzo, on the coast of Sicily, in February, 1807, under the command of Major General Alexander Mackenzie Fraser, Colonel of the Seventy-Eighth regiment, and landed at Aboukir on the 18th of March. On the 21st of March, Alexandria was occupied by the British troops, and it is a singular coincidence that it was the anniversary of the battle fought near there in the year 1801, when the gallant General Sir Ralph Abercromby received the wound which terminated his honourable career.

On the 27th of March, 1807, a force of fifteen hundred men, of which the Thirty-First regiment formed part, was detached under the command of Major-General Wauchope to Rosetta. The troops arrived before the city on the 31st of March, and not having been impeded in their progress to the environs, entered the place. The Thirty-First regiment marched into Rosetta, while the grenadier battalion occupied a high sandy mound without the city.

Rosetta is situated upon a slight eminence, commanding a view of the River Nile and the fertile lands of the Delta; the streets are somewhat wider than the generality of Egyptian towns, and planted here and there with trees. The houses are high, the lower half of each being a dead wall, with a small door, leading into a narrow passage, well secured with bolts and bars of iron. The chambers are above, with trellised windows projecting over the streets. The Turks had garrisoned their houses, and remaining quiet, allowed the British to continue their march until some way into the town, when through the loop-holes they had constructed on purpose, and their trellised windows, a destructive and unexpected fire was opened upon the column.

The troops, although placed in a most trying and perilous situation, behaved extremely well, and after having suffered very materially in killed and wounded, retired to Aboukir, from whence they returned to Alexandria.

Major-General Wauchope, who commanded the force, was killed; the Thirty-First regiment had Captain John Robertson, three sergeants, three drummers, and sixty-nine rank and file killed; Captain Patrick Dowdall, Lieutenants Edward Knox, Peter Fearon, John Thornton,—Sladden, and Francis Ryan, Ensign Richard Kirby, seven sergeants, one drummer, and one hundred and twenty-nine rank and file wounded. Lieutenant Sladden subsequently died of his wounds.

Brigadier-General the Honourable Robert Meade (Lieutenant-Colonel of the Thirty-First), the second in command, was also severely wounded.

Major-General Fraser finding that a famine would be the consequence of the British remaining at Alexandria, without the occupation of Rosetta, detached another body of troops, amounting to two thousand five hundred men, under Brigadier-General the Honourable William Stewart, to reduce the place. The force consisted of a detachment of Royal Artillery, a detachment of the Twentieth Light Dragoons, light infantry battalion, first battalion of the Thirty-Fifth regiment, second battalion of the Seventy-Eighth regiment, the Baron De Roll's regiment, and a detachment of seamen. A large Turkish force coming down the Nile from Cairo, the troops were compelled to retire, fighting all the way to Alexandria.

A formidable force now approached Alexandria, and Major-General Fraser sent a flag of truce offering to evacuate Egypt, on condition that the British prisoners should be liberated. The proposal was readily accepted, and on the 19th of September the British troops embarked for Sicily, where they arrived on the 16th of October.

The first battalion of the Thirty-First regiment embarked from Sicily for Malta, on the 17th of September, 1808, where it remained until August 1810, when it returned to Sicily.

On the 17th of August, 1810, the first battalion landed at Messina, and remained in garrison in the citadel until April, 1811, when Lieut.-General Lord 1811 William Bentinck, being about to proceed to the eastern coast of Spain, sent it to Malta, in order that a stronger corps might be drawn from that island, the Thirty-First having been reduced considerably in numbers while stationed in the Mediterranean. The battalion landed at Malta on the 18th of April, but the force left in Sicily being found insufficient, four companies were immediately recalled, and on the 22nd of April re-embarked for Messina; a few months afterwards the headquarters were ordered back to Sicily, and on the 28th of August joined the detached companies, when the battalion was once more united in Sicily.

About this period the British authorities in Sicily detected the traces of a conspiracy set on foot the year before by the Queen of Naples, who, it is said, had proposed a scheme to Napoleon for massacring the English. A new constitution was established in Sicily, upon the model of that of Great Britain, under the auspices of Lieut.-General Lord William Bentinck, who had been appointed Captain-General of the island, and the queen was sent into retirement.

In November, 1812, the grenadier company of the Thirty-First regiment embarked from Sicily for the east coast of Spain, under Lieut.-General Frederick Maitland, and landed at Alicant on the 2nd of December. In April, 1813, it returned to Sicily, where it arrived in May.

The first battalion of the Thirty-First regiment remained in garrison in the citadel of Messina until towards the end of 1813, when, in consequence of disturbances at Palermo, the capital of Sicily, which threatened to spread, the troops were detached to various central positions. The Thirty-First, by a detour, marched upon Castro Giovanni, and remained there until January, 1814, when the battalion returned to Messina.

On the 28th of March, 1814, the battalion embarked at Molazzo. as part of an expedition destined for the shores of Italy, under Lieut.-General Lord William Bentinck. In the beginning of April the first division of the army arrived off the coast above and below the city of Genoa, and threatened a descent upon Voltri, rather to engage the attention of the enemy, however, in that quarter, than for any other purpose.

On the 5th of April the second division of the Anglo-Sicilian Army disembarked at Leghorn, and marched directly upon Sestri. The French reinforced that place to protect the coast batteries, and prevent the British communicating with the people of the mountains, who were ready to rise against the French. The two British divisions had united, and attacked the enemy, on the 8th of April, at Sestri; the battle lasted throughout the day, and in the night the French General Ronger St. Victor retired towards Recco, taking up his position in rear of Rafallo, where he left his advanced guard; a third British division, in which was the first battalion of the Thirty-First, hovered about the coast, and made some attempts to land fresh troops, but was prevented by the enemy's detachments at Recco.

On the 9th and 10th of April the squadron cannonaded Recco, but was obliged to stand out again; in the night of the 10th General Pègot, who had arrived to relieve General Ronger St. Victor, retired, and occupied, on the 11th of April, 1814, a position at Mount Fascia. The English squadron and transports had all arrived before Genoa, and a detachment from the divisions on shore had been able to communicate with the native levies at Fontana Buona.

On the 12th of April the position of Mount Fascia was attacked, and, after a hard day's contest, General Pègot fell back in the night, and took up another strong position at La Sturla, on the heights of Albaro, his right on the sea being covered by a battery of four pieces of artillery, and his left resting on Fort Richelieu. The remainder of the British Army disembarked at Nervi, and immediately attacked the enemy on the heights of Albaro, on the 13th of April.

The Thirty-First, under the command of Colonel Bruce, belonged to this division, and, with the 8th battalion of the Line of the King's German Legion, dashed in among the enemy the instant of their debarkation, notwithstanding the intersected and difficult nature of the ground, which assisted so materially the obstinate defence of the French. Meanwhile the light company of the Thirty-First, under Captain Nunn, had carried the battery which covered the enemy's right, with conspicuous bravery, and dismounted the four guns upon it under a galling fire of musketry and artillery from another battery near that captured.

The Thirty-First had Captains Stewart and Cruice, three sergeants, one drummer, and thirty-six rank and file wounded; one sergeant and thirteen rank and file killed.

The following extract from Division Orders, dated La Sturla, 14th of April, 1814, bears testimony to the conduct of the corps:—

> The conduct of the troops in the long contested action of yesterday, at La Sturla, was most honourable to them, and Major-General Montresor feels the greatest satisfaction in doing justice to their merits, by publicly declaring his high sense of their persevering gallantry in surmounting the numberless obstacles which the broken and intersected nature of the country presented, in every step, to their advance, whilst it afforded the

best shelter to the enemy, who, well accustomed to his ground, defended it with the greatest obstinacy.

However justly entitled the whole may be to individual distinction, it nevertheless would be unjust not to notice, in particular, the ardour and spirited skill in which the Royal Flotilla, and the detachments of the third Italian Levy, and of the second and third extra regiments, and Royal Marines, began the attack, and the very gallant manner in which the Thirty-First regiment, and the 8th King's German Legion, dashed in amongst the enemy after their debarkation, and the conspicuous bravery of the light company of the Thirty-First regiment, in carrying the battery on the left.

During the 14th and 15th of April the attacks upon the heights of Albaro were repeated, and on the 17th, while disaffection among the people was rapidly spreading in Genoa, the posts of St. Francisco and St. Martin d'Albaro were carried, and the French retired behind the Bizagno.

By the 18th of April the disaffection in Genoa had reached a crisis, and upon the following day the advance upon the city took place. The Thirty-First drove the enemy from a strong battery of ten brass guns and two 13½-inch brass mortars, without sustaining any loss.

During the night of the 19th of April, 1814, a convention was signed; on the morning of the 21st, the enemy marched out of the city and evacuated all his posts. On the 22nd the headquarters of the Thirty-First were within the city of Genoa, when the commander-in-chief, Lieut.-General Lord William Bentinck, issued the order from which the following extract is taken:—

Headquarters, Genoa, 24th April, 1814.
The Commander of the Forces has much satisfaction in witnessing the zeal and gallantry evinced by the whole of the troops under his orders in the late operations, which have led to the possession of this important fortress; and he has not failed to represent their conduct in the most favourable terms to His Majesty's government.

Major-General Montresor has particularly reported to him the great assistance he received from Brigadier-General Roth, Colonel Bruce, and Lieut.-Colonel Travers.

The Commander of the Forces himself observed the very gallant and successful attack made by the Third Italian regiment, under the orders of Lieut.-Colonel Ciravignac, and favourable reports have been made to him of the conduct of the light company of the Twenty-First regiment, commanded by Captain Renny, the light company of the Thirty-First, under Captain Nunn, and the light company of the Second Estero regiment, under Captain-Lieutenant Fulghier.

On the 27th of April the first battalion of the Thirty-First sailed with a force for the island of Corsica; when the troops arrived opposite Ajaccio, that place capitulated. The Thirty-First regiment then sailed for Bastia (the birthplace of Napoleon), and landing there on the 11th of May, remained until the 24th of June following, when it embarked for Sicily, and again went into garrison in the citadel of Messina, on the 18th of July, 1814.

In the meantime the brilliant successes gained over the French in the Peninsula and South of France, by the troops under the Duke of Wellington, in which the second battalion of the Thirty-First regiment bore a prominent part, led to a treaty of peace with France; Napoleon retired to Elba, which island was ceded to him in full sovereignty for life, with a pension payable from the revenues of France; and on the 3rd of May, 1814, Louis XVIII. entered Paris, and ascended the throne of his ancestors.

On the 24th of October, 1814, the second battalion of the Thirty-First regiment was disbanded at Portsmouth, and the officers and men fit for service were transferred to the first battalion, with which they were incorporated on the 6th of May, 1815, at Messina.

In commemoration of the services of the second battalion during the Peninsular War, the Thirty-First regiment has received the Royal Authority to bear on the Regimental Colour and Appointments, the words "Talavera," "Albuhera," "Vittoria," "Pyrenees," "Nivelle," "Nive," "Orthes," and "Peninsula."

Although the first and second battalions of the Thirty-First regiment were employed in different countries, yet they were engaged in the promotion of the same interests, namely, the restoration of the exiled families of the House of Bourbon to the thrones of their ancestors; the achievements of the second battalion were in the most distinguished arena, but the first battalion, although it was stationed among the pastoral beauties of Sicily, and the luxurious towns of Italy, maintained its discipline and character, besides adding honours to those formerly acquired on the field of battle, whenever, as on the heights of Albaro, an opportunity had offered.

The peace of Europe was again to be disturbed. The French Army retained a chivalrous veneration for Napoleon, who returned from Elba, landed at Cannes, in Provence, on the 1st of March, 1815, and was joined by his former troops. Louis XVIII. withdrew from Paris to Ghent, and Napoleon assumed his former dignity of Emperor of the French.

Marshal Murat. the brother-in-law of Napoleon, by whom in 1808 he had been made King of Naples, upon Joseph Bonaparte being constituted King of Spain, had, in January, 1814, signed a treaty with England, and engaged to co-operate with the allies against France. Napoleon's triumphal return to France caused Murat to espouse his cause, and he at once commenced hostilities against Austria, issuing a proclamation asserting the independence of Italy. Naples was thereupon invested by the Austrians, while an English squadron entered the port and acted in co-operation.

The allied powers, however, refused to acknowledge the sovereignty of Napoleon, and determined on his dethronement.

These events caused the Thirty-First regiment to be embarked at Melazzo for Naples, where it arrived on the 25th of May. The city had capitulated to the British fleet, under Admiral Lord Exmouth, and the troops landed to hold possession until the restoration of order in the kingdom, and Ferdinand IV. should be reinstated on the throne of the Two Sicilies. After an exile of nine years, this sovereign entered his capital on the 17th of June; on the following day the hopes of Bonaparte were crushed by his defeat on the memorable field of Waterloo, which victory triumphantly closed the campaign; and on the 8th of July Louis XVIII. re-entered Paris, and the Bourbon government was restored.

In the beginning of July the Thirty-First had sailed from the Bay of Naples for Genoa, and remained there to support the arrangements for restoring the Sardinian dominions to their original state.

Bonaparte was subsequently compelled to surrender himself a prisoner on the 15th of July to Captain Maitland, commanding the *Bellerophon* ship of war, and the island of St. Helena was afterwards appointed for his residence. Murat's career was equally brief; he was driven from Italy, and withdrew to Corsica, from which island he made a rash descent on the coast of Calabria. After a sharp action he and his followers were taken prisoners. Murat was tried by a military commission, and shot on the 15th of October.

In February, 1816, the Thirty-First regiment embarked for Malta, and remained in that island until June, 1818, when it proceeded to England, and landed at Deal on the 22nd of July.

The Second Battalion

Napoleon Bonaparte, upon being raised in May 1804 to the dignity of Emperor of the French, increased his immense preparations to carry into effect his project for the invasion of England, that he might, by one great effort, crush the power of the British people, who appeared as a barrier to his ambitious designs. This menace of invasion had aroused the spirit of the British nation; patriotic enthusiasm pervaded all ranks; and among the measures of defence adopted by the Government was the introduction of the "Additional Force Act" which was passed on the 14th of July 1804.

Under this Act of Parliament, a second battalion was added to the Thirty-First regiment, which was to be formed of men raised in the county of Chester for limited service.

The second battalion was embodied by July 1805, and in October it proceeded from Chester to Winchester, where the first battalion was stationed.

After the first battalion had embarked for Sicily in April 1806, the second battalion continued at Winchester until June following, when it proceeded to Gosport.

On the 8th of January 1807, the second battalion embarked at Gosport for Guernsey, where it arrived on the 15th of that month. In May 1807, the battalion proceeded to Ireland, and was stationed at Limerick.

In March 1808, the battalion was removed from Limerick to Dublin.

Important events had in the meantime occurred on the Continent, which occasioned the second battalion of the Thirty-First regiment to be ordered on active service. Napoleon, having reduced Germany to submission to his will, and forced Russia to accede to his decrees, next attempted the subjugation of Spain and Portugal. The Spaniards and Portuguese rose in arms to assert their national rights, the French emperor having conferred the crown of Spain on his brother Joseph, who relinquished the throne of Naples in favour of Marshal Murat.

In the summer of 1808, Portugal was delivered by a British army under Lieut.-General Sir Arthur Wellesley; and in the autumn Lieut.-General Sir John Moore received orders to advance with a body of British troops from Portugal into the heart of Spain; at the same time several regiments were embarked from the United Kingdom to cooperate in the enterprise.

The second battalion of the Thirty-First, which had proceeded in August to Fermoy, marched on the 8th of September to Monkstown for embarkation, and sailed in a few days afterwards to Falmouth, where a fleet was assembling with a force for service, the command of the troops being held by Lieut.-General Sir David Baird. In a short time, the fleet sailed, and arrived in the Bay of Corunna on the 23rd of October. The Thirty-First did not, however, land with the army, the battalion being despatched to Lisbon, where it arrived on the 5th of November.

Lieut.-General Sir John Cradock, who commanded in Portugal at this period, detached some regiments towards the frontier, with a view of reinforcing Lieut.-General Sir John Moore in Spain. The Thirty-First, being one of the corps destined for this service, marched with a force under the command of Brigadier-General Richard Stewart from Lisbon, on the 18th of December, upon Castello Branco, where the battalion arrived in ten days.

The communication with Lieut.-General Sir John Moore being at this period suddenly interrupted, Brigadier-General Stewart was ordered to halt, and unfavourable intelligence being received from Spain, Lieut.-General Sir John Cradock determined to concentrate his army near Lisbon, and the further advance was, therefore, countermanded.

The second battalion of the Thirty-First, and the other corps of the division, commenced their march to the rear on the 1st of January 1809. On arrival at Santarem, the intelligence of Sir John Moore's advance upon Sahagun had reached headquarters, and the anticipated danger being thus drawn from the frontiers of Portugal, Brigadier-General Stewart was again ordered to halt. His headquarters continued at Santarem, and the Thirty-First occupied cantonments in the neighbourhood of Bucellas. A month's march in incessant rain had seriously damaged the appointments, and the men being indifferently provided with shoes, rendered a rest in this pleasant quarter of infinite benefit.

In the meanwhile, the army under Lieut.-General Sir John Moore had continued its retreat over two hundred and fifty miles of mountainous country, constantly repulsing the attacks of the enemy. The British Army arrived at Corunna on the 11th of January, being closely followed by Marshal Soult, who occupied a position on a height above the town, in order to make an attack on the troops while proceeding to embark. This operation commenced on the 16th of January, and the French descending from the heights in three columns, a sanguinary action ensued. Lieut.-General Sir John Moore received a mortal wound from a cannon-ball, and his country was deprived of an officer, who, both in his professional and private character, had acquired universal esteem and admiration. Lieut.-General Sir David Baird lost an arm, and the command devolved on Lieut.-General Sir John Hope, who vigorously maintained the action, the British remaining masters of the field. The embarkation for England was effected on the following night, no further molestation being offered by the enemy.

No change was made in the disposition of the army in Portugal until the middle of March, when Lieut.-General Sherbrooke, and Major-General John Randoll McKenzie, with their corps arrived. The army was then drawn together between Lumiar and Sacavem, in which position it encamped until toward the end of April, when Lieut.-General Sir John Cradock commenced his advance towards Spain on the 24th of that month; and when Lieut.-General Sir Arthur Wellesley, who had arrived at Lisbon with reinforcements, assumed the command of the army, the force was assembled at Leiria. The first object of Lieut.-General Sir Arthur Wellesley was to dislodge Marshal Soult from Oporto, and he accordingly marched towards that city at the end of April.

A corps of British and Portuguese was detached, previous to Sir Arthur Wellesley's march upon Oporto, under Major-General McKenzie, to watch the right bank of the Tagus in observation of Marshal Victor in Estremadura. The second battalion of the Thirty-First joined this army, and remained posted at Thomar until after the famous passage of the Douro by the British general, and the fall of Oporto, which compelled Marshal Soult to retreat.

In the month of June the second battalion of the Thirty-First was at Cortiçada with Major-General McKenzie's headquarters, and in that officer's division reached Placentia, whence on the 17th of July it commenced its march to Oropesa, where it arrived on the 20th. A junction with the Spanish Army under General Cuesta was effected here, and on the 22nd the advanced guards, to which the Thirty-First belonged, moved forward to the attack on the French posts at Talavera. The enemy's position was turned by the British cavalry and infantry, while the Spanish General drove the French on in front. On the 25th, in consequence of General Cuesta having followed the enemy, two divisions of infantry were sent across the Alberche to Casa Legas. The second battalion of the Thirty-First was in that commanded by Major-General McKenzie, and was brigaded with the Twenty-Eighth and Forty-Fifth regiments.

On the 27th of July, when General Cuesta had retreated from Alcabon under cover of Lieut.-General Sherbrooke's divisions, Lieut.-General Sir Arthur Wellesley withdrew to the position of Talavera, leaving Major-General McKenzie on the Alberche to protect the movement. When the French, on the 27th of July, crossed this river, Major-General McKenzie's division was posted near the Casa des Salinas, his infantry in the forest, and cavalry on the plain.

The attack was somewhat sudden, and the Thirty-First and Eighty-Seventh regiments, which were in the wood on the right of the Alberche, sustained some loss. As the enemy increased his numbers on the British side of the river, Major-General McKenzie fell back gradually, and entering the position by the left of the combined army, took up his ground in a second line, in rear of the foot guards. In the dusk of the evening the enemy commenced his attack on the British left, but failed; in the night the attack was repeated, and on the morning of the 28th of July the French renewed the attack on the height on the British left, and were again repulsed with considerable loss. After a pause of some hours the attacks were renewed upon the whole British front, and the action became general. Brigadier-General Alexander Campbell's division, on the British right, sustained the assault of the enemy's fourth corps, assisted by Major-General McKenzie's brigade.

> The English regiments, putting the French skirmishers aside, met the advancing columns with loud shouts, and breaking in on their front, and lapping their flanks with fire, and giving no respite, pushed them back with a terrible carnage. Ten guns were taken; but as General Campbell prudently forbore pursuit, the French rallied on their supports, and made a show of attacking again: vain attempt! The British artillery and musketry played too vehemently upon their masses, and a Spanish regiment of cavalry charging on their flank at the same time, the whole retired in disorder, and the victory was secured in that quarter.—Major-General Sir William Napier's *History of the Peninsular War.*

The ten captured guns remained in possession of the British;—Major General John Randall McKenzie was killed;—and the second battalion of the Thirty-First regiment, under Major John Williams Watson, conducted itself in such a manner as to merit notice in the despatch, as well as approbation in General Orders. Major Watson received a medal, and was afterwards promoted to the rank of Lieutenant-Colonel for his conduct on this occasion.

The Thirty-First, in the actions of the 27th and 28th of July, had Captain William Lodge, two sergeants, and forty-two rank and file killed; Captains Nicolls and Coleman,—Lieutenants George Beamish, Adderley Beamish, and Girdlestone,—Ensigns Gamble and Soden,—Assistant Surgeon Edwards,—eight sergeants, and one hundred and eighty-two rank and file, wounded. Most of the wounded fell into the hands of the French, on the abandonment of Talavera afterwards by the Spanish General. Assistant Surgeon Edwards, who was left in charge of the wounded, died shortly afterwards. The news of the brilliant victory of Talavera, gained over the French army commanded by Joseph Bonaparte in person, excited great joy in England, and Lieut.-General Sir Arthur Wellesley was raised to the peerage by the title of Viscount Wellington. The Royal Authority was afterwards given for the Thirty-First to bear the word "Talavera" on the Regimental Colour and Appointments, to commemorate the distinguished conduct of the second battalion on that memorable occasion.

After the battle of the 28th of July, the second battalion was posted to Major-General Tilson's brigade, in the division commanded by Major-General Rowland (afterwards Viscount) Hill; and on the 3rd of August marched from Talavera, in order to oppose the French, who had entered Estremadura by Placentia.

On the 3rd of September, the head-quarters arrived at Badajoz, and the army was distributed about Elvas, Campo Mayor, and other places, the Thirty-First being in the division cantoned at Montejo. The troops had suffered greatly on the march from Talavera, generally from dysentery, brought on by bad food, fatigue, and exposure. When the second battalion had rested awhile in its position, the sickness that had been kept off in a great measure by the previous excitement, now visited the men severely, and a considerable number died.

When Viscount Wellington broke up from the Guadiana in the month of December, and crossed the Tagus, he left Lieut.-General Hill, who had been appointed to serve on the Staff in the Peninsula as a Lieut.-General, after the Battle of Talavera, with a force of ten thousand men, British and Portuguese, at Abrantes. Among the former was the second battalion of the Thirty-First; it continued at that place until

February 1810, when Lieut.-General Hill, on the approach of Marshal Mortier on Badajoz, marched to Portalegre, and occupied that strong position. He made a move on the 23rd of April through the Sierra de St. Marmede, which had the desired effect of relieving General O'Donnell at Albuquerque, the enemy retiring to Merida. Lieut.-General Hill was once more at Portalegre on the 26th of April, and on the 15th of May he again quitted his cantonment, by which movement he disengaged Badajoz from the attention of the enemy, who had made a reconnaissance on the 12th of that place, and relieved General Ballasteros, returning in a few days afterwards to his old position.

During the continuance of the division at Portalegre, it was always on the alert, owing to General Regnier's movements in Estremadura. In the beginning of July, Lieut.-General Hill concentrated his corps at Campo Mayor, previously to an expedition into Estremadura in conjunction with the Marquis de Romana. General Regnier had, however, frustrated this plan, by quitting Merida on the 10th of July, and marching upon Alconete and Almaraz, effected the passage of the Tagus on the 16th. Lieut.-General Hill made a parallel movement, and crossing the river at Vilha Velha, was at Castello Branco on the 21st; he encamped at Sarzedas, in front of the Sobreira Formosa, remaining some time in observation between the Estrella and the Tagus.

Upon Marshal Massena concentrating his force for the invasion of Portugal, Lieut.-General Hill fell back from his position at Sarzedas, and on the 21st of August, arrived on the Alva. On the 26th, the Thirty-First, in Lieut.-General Hill's corps, crossed the Mondego, arrived on the *Sierra de Busaco*, and was posted on the right, across the road leading over the mountain ridge to Peña Cova, but the battalion was not engaged in the action.

When General Regnier attacked the position held by the third and fifth divisions, Lieut.-General Hill withdrew towards his left to support them; it was unnecessary however, these divisions having repulsed the enemy, and he therefore continued in his original position.

After the Battle of Busaco, fought on the 27th of September, the army withdrew from the Sierra, and Lieut.-General Hill's division marched on Thomar, arriving there on the 4th of October; whence continuing its retreat by Santarem, it took up its ground, on the 8th, on the right of the Torres Vedras lines at Alhandra, on the right of the Tagus, in which position the second battalion of the Thirty-First had several skirmishes with the enemy, without sustaining much loss. The battalion remained at Alhandra, opposite which was the second

French corps under General Regnier.

On the 17th of November, the second division crossed the Tagus at Villada upon Abrantes, where the French were in retreat. Upon Marshal Massena taking up a position at Santarem, it halted at Chamako, where the headquarters were stationed; the troops being so distributed as to have an eye to the enemy, and prevent his crossing to the south of the Tagus. Lieut.-General Hill returned to England on account of ill health in December, and Marshal Sir William Carr (now Viscount) Beresford succeeded him in the command of his division, which amounted to fourteen thousand men, British and Portuguese.

The hostile armies remained in the same positions until the beginning of March 1811, when Marshal Massena broke up from Santarem, and Major-General the Honourable William Stewart, with a body of troops, of which the Thirty-First formed part, crossed the Tagus at Abrantes, and moved to Thomar, while Marshal Beresford remained at Barla, and did not join in the pursuit of Marshal Massena.

Towards the end of March, Sir William Beresford arrived at Portalegre with twenty thousand infantry, two thousand cavalry, and eighteen guns, with orders to relieve Campo Mayor, and besiege Olivenza and Badajoz. The first object was effected on the 25th. of March; it was an affair of cavalry only. On the 6th of April, the passage of the Guadiana took place at Jurumenha, and the army occupied a position on a strong range of hills. On the 9th of April, Olivenza was summoned, and not surrendering the army encamped round it. General Latour Maubourg having retired to Llerena, Marshal Beresford leaving the fourth division, with Colonel Madden's cavalry, opposite Olivenza, took post on the 11th at Albuhera, the infantry being on the 16th drawn nearer to Badajoz, which place was invested on the 8th of May.

On the 8th and 10th of May, the French made two sorties, but were driven back with considerable loss. Marshal Soult's approach to relieve Badajoz having been ascertained, the siege was raised on the night of the 12th, and moving to Albuhera, the British were in position on the 15th of May.

The second battalion of the Thirty-First was on the left of Lieut.-Colonel Colborne's brigade, in the division under Major-General the Honourable William Stewart, which was drawn up, in one line, behind the village of Albuhera; its right on a commanding hill, over which the Valverde road passed; its left on the road to Badajoz.

On the morning of the 16th of May, the grand attack was made by the French on the right of the position, and in a line at right angles to it: this point was contested by the Spaniards without success,—they gave way, and the French columns pushing on, seized the crown of the hill, and bringing up their reserves, established their batteries in position on it. At this moment Major-General the Honourable William Stewart brought forward Lieut.-Colonel Colborne's brigade, and arrived with it at the foot of the hill, while all was in confusion above. The Major-General rushed on in open column of companies, attempting to form his line in succession as the battalions arrived. The Thirty-First, the left of the brigade, was still in column, when four regiments of hussars and lancers, which had been concealed by the heavy rain falling at the time, passed by the right flank to the rear of the line.

> One battalion only (the Thirty-First) being still in column, escaped the storm, and maintained its ground, while the French horsemen, riding violently over everything else, penetrated to all parts.—*History of the Peninsular War* by Major-General Sir William Napier.

Major-General the Honourable William Lumley sent some squadrons of cavalry to take the attention of the lancers, but the Thirty-First continued to hold the height, while the Spaniards would not advance, and Marshal Soult still kept his columns together on the point he had assailed. Major-General Hoghton's brigade coming up in good order, under Major-General the Honourable William Stewart, and being soon afterwards reinforced by a portion of the fourth division, relieved the second battalion of the thirty-first from the difficulty of its position.

The Thirty-First had two sergeants and twenty-six rank and file killed; and Captains Fleming and Knox, Lieutenants Butler, Gethen, and Bolton; Ensigns Wilson and Nicholson; four sergeants, and one hundred and sixteen rank and file, wounded.

Major George Guy Carleton L'Estrange, who commanded the battalion, at the Battle of Albuhera, was promoted to the rank of Lieut.-Colonel in the army for his conduct on that day, and received a medal. Viscount Wellington alluded to his gallantry in the following terms:—

> There is one officer, Major L'Estrange, of the Thirty-First, whom I must recommend, in the strongest manner, for promotion in some way or other. *After the other parts of the same brigade were swept off by the cavalry, this little battalion alone held its ground against all the 'colonnes en masse.'*

Captain Peter Fearon, of the Thirty-First, distinguished himself on the same day in command of the Lusitanian legion, and received a medal for his conduct.

The Royal Authority was afterwards given for the Thirty-First to bear the word "Albuhera" on the regimental colour and appointments, to commemorate the distinguished conduct of the second battalion on that memorable occasion.

The army was again in position during the 17th of May, the enemy appearing to meditate another attack; the remainder of the fourth division, however, arrived by forced marches from Jurumenha, and on the 18th Marshal Soult retreated, followed by Marshal Beresford, who left the Portuguese to make a show of investing Badajoz. The infantry had no affair with the enemy during his retreat; and when he assumed a position at Llerena, the operations terminated.

Major-General Hill at this period rejoined from England, and the second siege of Badajoz commenced on the 30th of May.

The second battalion of the Thirty-First continued under Lieut.-General Hill, to which rank he was promoted on the 4th of June 1811, in the covering army, which was posted between Merida and Albuhera. Having been much reduced in the late action, it was formed, with the sixty-sixth regiment, into a Provisional Battalion, under the command of Lieut.-Colonel Colborne.

When Marshal Soult advanced, and the siege of Badajoz was raised, the covering army was once more concentrated on the position of Albuhera. The French Marshal did not, however, attack; on the 17th of June, the British crossed the Guadiana, and prepared for the probability of an engagement with the united corps of Marshals Marmont and Soult. In July, the British were relieved from their presence, and the commander-in-chief, Viscount Wellington, leaving Lieut.-General Hill to watch Estremadura, at Portalegre, Villa Viciosa. and Estremos, with ten thousand men, put the rest of the army into quarters near the Tagus.

The Thirty-First continued with Lieut.-General Hill in the second division: this part of the army was constantly on the alert, but nothing very important occurred until October.

On the 9th of October, Lieut.-General Hill's force was concentrated behind Campo Mayor, and on the 22nd marched to drive Marshal Girard from Caçeres: at daylight on the 28th of October, the British General surprised the French Marshal at Arroyo dos Molinos, in which brilliant affair the second battalion of the Thirty-First was present.

The army returned to its cantonments about Portalegre immediately afterwards, and remained in them until the 24th and 25th of December, when it moved upon Merida, and arrived there on the 30th to surprise General Dombrouski, and attack General Drouet. They both retired, abandoning magazines of wheat, and Lieut.-General Hill took up his cantonments at Merida on the 6th of January, 1812.

Immediately afterwards Lieut.-General Hill fell back upon the frontiers of Portugal, while the grand army was investing Ciudad Rodrigo, and occupied Portalegre.

In March, Badajoz was invested for the third time, and Lieut.-General Sir Rowland Hill's (Lieut.-General Rowland Hill was nominated a Knight of the Bath on the 22nd of February, 1812), corps again formed part of the covering army. He halted at Almendralejos, while Lieut.-General Sir Thomas Graham (afterwards Lord Lynedoch) took post at Zafra. Lieut. General Sir Rowland Hill's division then moved forward, and took post at Medellin. When the breaches at Badajoz were nearly practicable, Marshal Soult, having effected a junction with Generals Drouot and Daricau, advanced to relieve it. Viscount Wellington thereupon determined to fight him at Albuhera. Lieut.-General Sir Thomas Graham then fell back towards that place, and Lieut.-General Sir Rowland Hill having destroyed the bridge at Merida, marched from the Upper Guadiana to Talavera Real. Marshal Soult did not however advance in time, and Badajoz was taken on the 6th of April.

After the fall of Badajoz, when Viscount Wellington marched towards Beira, two divisions of British infantry, in one of which was the second battalion of the Thirty-First, remained with Lieut.-General Sir Rowland Hill in Estremadura, to cover Badajoz during the re-establishment of its works. Nothing occurred in the army until the 12th of May, when six thousand men, with twelve field-pieces, crossed the Guadiana at Merida, and joining the battering train and pontoons, formed the force destined to surprise the French at Almaraz.

The Thirty-First remained in position on the Guadiana, while the expedition proceeded to attack the French works on the Bridge at Almaraz, on the Tagus, which were captured on the 19th of May. The bridge having been destroyed, and the communication between the several divisions of the French army rendered more difficult, the British troops returned to the south of the Guadiana.

A great part of June was passed in operations against General Drouet, until he was reinforced on the 18th of that month with General Barrois's division of infantry, and two divisions of cavalry. Hereupon Lieut.-General Sir Rowland Hill fell back gradually to Albuhera, and took up a position on the former field, awaiting an attack. The enemy did not advance, and on the 2nd of July, Lieut.-General Sir Rowland Hill broke up from Albuhera, and moved upon General Drouet, who retired towards Cordova. At the end of July, Lieut.-General Sir Rowland Hill was at Llerena, and the second battalion of the Thirty-First regiment, in Brigadier-General Byng's brigade, was detached to Merida. General Drouet made a demonstration, but no action of infantry ensued.

After the victory gained by the army under Viscount Wellington on the 22nd of July at Salamanca, the troops under Lieut.-General Sir Rowland Hill penetrated the Spanish provinces: during the month of August they were engaged in the pursuit of General Drouet, and in the beginning of October they were on the Tagus, between Aranjuez and Toledo.

While the army under the Marquis of Wellington, which title was conferred upon him after the victory of Salamanca, was engaged in the siege of the Castle of Burgos, the second battalion of the thirty-first regiment remained at Aranjuez. In consequence of the necessity of raising the siege of Burgos, and retreating, Lieut.-General Sir Rowland Hill broke up from his ground on the Tagus, to effect a junction with the grand army, which commenced its retrograde movement from Burgos on the 21st of October.

On the 30th of October, Lieut.-General Sir Rowland Hill, having taken up a position of defence on the Jarama, was pressed by the enemy, who attacked the bridge of Aranjuez. The French were repulsed by Colonel Skerrett, with the Forty-Seventh (of which he was the Lieutenant-Colonel), and part of the Ninety-Fifth regiment, now the Rifle Brigade. The retreat continued without molestation: and on the 8th of November, the troops under Lieut.-General Sir Rowland Hill were at Alba, while the Marquis of Wellington occupied the heights of San Christoval. The brigade of the second division, in which the second battalion of the Thirty-First was posted, being in the neighbourhood of the fords of Encinas.

On the 14th of November, the enemy passed the river near that place, and the Marquis of Wellington moved with the second division to attack him, while the remainder of the troops were ordered towards the Arapiles in the evening. No engagement occurred. The enemy fortified himself at Mozarbes, on the ground he had taken up the night before, and moved bodies of cavalry and infantry to the communication with Ciudad Rodrigo. The superiority of numbers on the part of the French caused the British Army to continue its march to Ciudad Rodrigo, which it reached on the 19th of November. Thus ended the retreat from Burgos. The men had suffered greatly on the march and required rest; the enemy had pressed the retreat closely with his cavalry, and made an attack upon the rear upon the passage of the Huebra; the roads were difficult, and in some parts impassable. The second battalion of the Thirty-First did not share in the hardships of the main retreat until it had crossed the Tormes.

Marshal Soult having retired to the Upper Tormes, towards the pass of Banos, it was reported that he intended to invade Portugal by the valley of the Tagus. Lieut.-General Sir Rowland Hill's division was therefore moved to the right as far as Robledo, to cover the pass of Perales. King Joseph, however, in December, took up his position for the winter, and the allied army was also distributed in quarters.

Lieut.-General Sir Rowland Hill's division occupied Coria and Placentia, the Thirty-First being cantoned in the latter place.

The allied army remained in cantonments until the month of May 1813; on the 10th of that month the second battalion of the thirty-first, in the second division, broke up from its winter quarters, and, forming a part of the right wing of the army, shared in the operations during the advance upon Burgos and Vittoria; in the plan for the action of the 21st of June, before Vittoria, Lieut.-General Sir Rowland Hill's corps, composed of Morillo's Spaniards, Sylveira's Portuguese, and the second British division, forming the right of the allied army, was to attack the enemy's left, and forcing the passage of the lower Zadora, at Puebla, assail the French on the heights beyond, entering the plain of Vittoria, by the defile of *la* Puebla.

The river was passed about ten o'clock a. m., and Morillo's Spaniards assailed the mountain with his first brigade; but meeting with much resistance on the heights, called up his second brigade, which, the French being also reinforced, vas supported by part of the second division, while Lieut.-General Sir Rowland Hill, with the rest, passed through the defile, and, seizing the village of Subijana de Alava, held his ground: he thus connected his own right with the troops on the mountain, and maintained this forward position, although the French made great efforts to dislodge the allies from this vantage-ground.

Meanwhile the fourth division crossed by the bridge of Nanclares.

The action on the British right was severe, and sustained with great gallantry. The French, being driven from all their defences, retreated with such precipitation towards Pampeluna as to abandon all their baggage, artillery, ammunition, military chests, and the court equipage of King Joseph, whose carriage being seized, he had barely time to escape on horseback. The defeat was the most complete that the French had experienced in Spain.

The *bâton* of Marshal Jourdan was taken, and the prince regent, in the name and behalf of His Majesty, appointed the Marquis of Wellington a Field Marshal. In a most flattering letter, the prince regent thus conferred the honour:—

> You have sent me among the trophies of your unrivalled fame, the staff of a French Marshal, and I send you in return that of England.

During part of the day, the second battalion of the Thirty-First was stationed to cover a brigade of guns: its loss was not very great, being one private killed, and thirteen wounded. Captain Girdlestone was the only officer of the Thirty-First who was wounded.

Lieut.-Colonel Leith received a medal for his conduct in command of the battalion, and the Royal Authority was afterwards given for the word "Vittoria" to be inscribed on :he Regimental Colour and Appointments of the Thirty-First regiment, to commemorate the gallantly of the second battalion in that battle.

The second battalion of the Thirty-First regiment shared in the pursuit of the enemy after his defeat at Vittoria, and, when the Marquis of Wellington marched on the 26th of June to intercept the French General Clausel, it remained with the other corps of the second division for the siege of Pampeluna.

Although the enemy had withdrawn his right and left into France, he maintained his centre in force in the rich valley of Bastan in, which afforded numerous strong: positions, and the troops under Lieut.-General Sir Rowland Hill, having been relieved from the blockade of Pampeluna, advanced to dislodge the French. On the 4th of July, and the three following days, General Gazan was driven from the valley of Bastan by the troops under Lieut.-General Sir Rowland Hill, and the positions abandoned by the enemy were occupied by the British. Major-General Byng's brigade, of which the Thirty-First formed part, with some Spanish corps under General Morillo, took possession of the Pass of Roncesvalles on the 7th of July. In this celebrated valley the

Thirty-First remained for a few days.

Marshal Soult having arrived at Bayonne on the 13th of July to command, as Lieutenant of the Emperor, the united French army of Spain, amounting to above seventy-eight thousand men, exclusive of garrisons, collected more than sixty thousand of his own left, and advanced on the 25th of July to force the Pass of Roncesvalles. The brigade which had been ordered to occupy the Pass, and of which the Thirty-First formed a part, kept the French in check for several hours, but was obliged to fall back, on perceiving that a strong body had succeeded in turning the position.

The Thirty-First had two privates killed, and three wounded, in the action on the 25th of July On the 28th and 30th of July, the battalion was engaged in the attack made upon the enemy on the heights in front of Pampeluna, and had Captain Girdlestone, Ensign Smith, and Quarter-Master McIntosh, together with thirty-three rank and file, wounded:—two rank and file were killed.

Lieut.-Colonel Leith received a clasp, in addition to his former medal, for his conduct on these occasions.

The Thirty-First regiment subsequently received the Royal Authority to bear the word "Pyrenees" on the Regimental Colour and Appointments, to commemorate the services of the second battalion in these several combats, which have been designated the "Battles of the Pyrenees."

On the 31st of July, Major-General Byng's brigade captured a large convoy near Elizondo, and made many prisoners.

The British troops resumed their position in the Pyrenees, awaiting the capture of St. Sebastian and Pampeluna. St. Sebastian was captured on the 31st of August, and on the 31st of October the French garrison of Pampeluna surrendered prisoners of war.

Pampeluna being captured, the right of the allied army, which had been employed in covering the blockade, became disengaged, and the British Commander looking down from the lofty Pyrenees on the well-guarded territory of France, resolved to carry the war into the heart of that country. The British army, early on the morning of the 10th of November, descended into the valleys on the French side; the division of which the Thirty-First formed part entered France by the Pass of Maya, having sustained some loss in the capture of one of the enemy's redoubts. Only one man belonging to the battalion was killed, but Captain Girdlestone and eleven rank and file were wounded. Marshal Soult's army was driven from his fortified position on the River Nivelle, and several guns and prisoners were captured. The French being pursued on the following day, retired to their fortified camp near Bayonne.

Captain Thomas Samuel Nicolls was promoted to the rank of Major in the army for his conduct on this day, and the Thirty-First afterwards received the Royal Authority to bear the word "Nivelle" on the Regimental Colour and Appointments, in testimony of the gallantry of the second battalion in that action.

The passage of the River Nive was effected on the 9th of December: the thirty-first passed over without the loss of a man, one sergeant only being wounded.

Lieut.-Colonel Leith received an additional clasp for his conduct on this occasion, and Captains Patrick Dowdall and Peter Fearon were promoted to the rank of Majors in the army.

On the 13th of December, the second battalion of the thirty-first regiment shared in the action at St. Pierre, near Bayonne, when the enemy abandoned two pieces of cannon, which were taken possession of by Captain Hemsworth's company.

The Marquis of Wellington, in his despatch dated St. Jean de Luz, 14th December 1813, thus alluded to the conduct of the brigade under Major-General John Byng, of which the Thirty-First formed part.

★★★★★★

Major-General Byng, the present General the Earl of Strafford, and Colonel of the Coldstream Guards, in consideration of his gallantry in the action of the 13th of December, 1813,—wherein he led his troops, under a most galling fire, to the assault of a strong height occupied in great force by the enemy, and having himself ascended the hill first with the colour of the Thirty-First regiment of Foot in his hand, he planted the colour upon the summit, and drove the enemy (far superior in numbers) down the ridge to the suburbs of St. Pierre,—received the Royal Authority on the 7th of July, 1815. to bear the following honourable augmentation, namely, "Over the arms of the family of Byng, in bend sinister, a representation of the valour of the Thirty-First regiment," and the following crest, namely, "Out of a second crown an arm embowed, grasping the colour of the aforesaid Thirty-First regiment, and, pendent from the wrist by a riband, the Gold Cross presented to him by His Majesty's command, as a mark of his royal approbation of his distinguished services," and in an *escrol* above the word

"Mouguerre," being the name of a height near the hamlet of St. Pierre.

******

I had great satisfaction, also, in observing the conduct of Major-General Byng's brigade of British infantry, supported by the fourth Portuguese brigade, under the command of Brigadier-General Buchan, in carrying an important height from the enemy on the right of our position, and maintaining it against all their efforts to regain it.

Two guns and some prisoners were taken from the enemy, who being beaten at all points, and having suffered considerable loss, were obliged to retire upon their entrenchment.

In a very interesting life of the late Viscount Hill, by the Reverend Edwin Sidney, A. M is the following account of the action at St. Pierre, near Bayonne.

"This great service was thus performed by Sir Rowland Hill. The enemy, who had failed in all their attempts with their whole force upon Lord Wellington's left, withdrew to their entrenchments on the night of December 12th, and passed a, large body of troops through the town of Bayonne. With these, on the morning of the 13th, they made a desperate attack on Sir Rowland Hill. This, as has appeared, was not unexpected; and Lord Wellington had placed at his disposal not only the sixth division, but the fourth division, and two brigades of the third. Soult's objects were to gain the bridge of St. Pierre, to make himself master of the road to St. Jean Pied de Port, and to break through the position of the allies. For these purposes he put forth his whole strength, and was completely vanquished. Even before the sixth division arrived. Sir Rowland Hill had repulsed him with prodigious loss; and although he skilfully availed himself of a high ground in retreating, he could not stand against the famous charge of General Byng, and was entirely defeated. It was a battle fought and won by the corps of Sir Rowland Hill alone and unaided. At the instant of victory Lord Wellington came up, and in the ecstasy of the moment of triumph, caught him by the hand, and said, 'Hill, the day is your own.'"

The Thirty-First had seven rank and file killed, and three sergeants, two drummers, and twenty-seven rank and file wounded.

Lieut.-Colonel Leith, who received a cross for his conduct, was slightly wounded. Ensign Hardy died of his wounds.

Brevet Major Peter Fearon, of the Thirty-First regiment, who commanded the fifth Portuguese Caçadores, received an additional distinction to the medal which had been granted him for the Battle of Albuhera.

The Thirty-First subsequently received the Royal Authority to bear on the Regimental colour the word "Nive," to commemorate the gallantry of the second battalion in the actions which ensued on the passage of that river.

No further actions occurred during the few remaining days of the year 1813; and the army occupied winter quarters.

Leaving their cantonments at the village of St. Pierre, the Thirty-First advanced with the troops under Lieut.-General Sir Rowland Hill, in the middle of February 1814, when the French corps, under General Harispe, were driven from Hellete, and afterwards forced from a position on the heights of Garris on the 15th of February. The battalion had one private killed, and six rank and file wounded. Brevet Major Peter Fearon, who commanded the Fifth Portuguese Caçadores, died of his wounds. The other officer wounded was Captain Knox, who was subsequently promoted to the brevet rank of major.

On the 27th of February, the second battalion of the Thirty-First, in Lieut.-General Sir Rowland Hill's division, crossed the Adour, on the right of Orthes, with the loss of only two rank and file wounded.

Lieut.-Colonel Leith gained another distinction, and the Thirty-First afterwards received the Royal Authority to bear the word "Orthes" on the Regimental Colour and Appointments, in commemoration of the conduct of the second battalion in that battle.

Advancing rapidly against the enemy, Lieut.-General Sir Rowland Hill engaged him at Aire, on which occasion the Thirty-First had Ensign Hardcastle (Captain in the Third Portuguese Caçadores) one sergeant, and two rank and file wounded.

On the 10th of April, the second battalion of the Thirty-First regiment was in action with the French in the suburbs of Toulouse and had one private wounded.

During the night of the 11th of April, the French Army evacuated Toulouse, and the white flag was hoisted. On the day following, the Marquis of Wellington entered the city amidst the acclamations of the inhabitants. In the afternoon of this day intelligence was received of the abdication of Napoleon; and had not the express been delayed on the journey by the French police, the sacrifice of many valuable lives would have been prevented. A disbelief in the truth of this intelligence occasioned much unnecessary bloodshed at Bayonne, the garrison of which made a desperate sortie on the 14th of April, and Lieut.-General Sir John Hope (afterwards Earl of Hopetoun) was wounded and taken prisoner. Major-General Andrew Hay was killed, and Major-General Stopford was wounded. This was the last action of the Peninsular War.

The advance of the Allied troops into the heart of France led to a Treaty of Peace, by which Louis XVIII. was restored to the throne of that kingdom, and Napoleon Bonaparte was permitted to reside at Elba, the sovereignty of that Island having been conferred upon him by the Allied Powers.

The war being ended, the second battalion of the Thirty-First regiment was ordered to return to England. It marched from Toulouse to Bourdeaux on the 3rd of June, and on the 12th of July embarked in the Rodney, disembarking on the 23rd at the Cove of Cork, whence it immediately marched to Middleton.

In commemoration of the services of the second battalion, the Thirty-First subsequently received the Royal Authority to bear the word "Peninsula," on the Regimental Colour and Appointments, in addition to the names of the several actions in which the second battalion had taken a prominent part, during the war in Spain from 1808 to 1814, namely, "Talavera," "Albuhera," "Vittoria," "Pyrenees," "Nivelle," "Nive," and "Orthes."

Lieut.-Colonel Alexander Leith was nominated a Knight Commander of the Order of the Bath for his conduct in command of the second battalion during the Peninsular war.

Lieut.-Colonel George Guy Carleton L'Estrange, who was promoted from major in the Thirty-First regiment, to the rank of Lieut.-Colonel in the Twenty-Sixth Regiment on the 15th of December 1812, was nominated a Companion of the Order of the Bath for his conduct while serving with the second battalion of the Thirty-First regiment.

On the 23rd of September, the second battalion proceeded to Portsmouth, where it was disbanded on the 24th of October 1814, the officers and men, fit for service, being transferred to the first battalion of the Thirty-First regiment, at that period stationed in Sicily.

ALSO FROM LEONAUR
AVAILABLE IN SOFTCOVER OR HARDCOVER WITH DUST JACKET

THE FALL OF THE MOGHUL EMPIRE OF HINDUSTAN by H. G. Keene—By the beginning of the nineteenth century, as British and Indian armies under Lake and Wellesley dominated the scene, a little over half a century of conflict brought the Moghul Empire to its knees.

LADY SALE'S AFGHANISTAN by Florentia Sale—An Indomitable Victorian Lady's Account of the Retreat from Kabul During the First Afghan War.

THE CAMPAIGN OF MAGENTA AND SOLFERINO 1859 by Harold Carmichael Wylly—The Decisive Conflict for the Unification of Italy.

FRENCH'S CAVALRY CAMPAIGN by J. G. Maydon—A Special Correspondent's View of British Army Mounted Troops During the Boer War.

CAVALRY AT WATERLOO by Sir Evelyn Wood—British Mounted Troops During the Campaign of 1815.

THE SUBALTERN by George Robert Gleig—The Experiences of an Officer of the 85th Light Infantry During the Peninsular War.

NAPOLEON AT BAY, 1814 by F. Loraine Petre—The Campaigns to the Fall of the First Empire.

NAPOLEON AND THE CAMPAIGN OF 1806 by Colonel Vachée—The Napoleonic Method of Organisation and Command to the Battles of Jena & Auerstädt.

THE COMPLETE ADVENTURES IN THE CONNAUGHT RANGERS by William Grattan—The 88th Regiment during the Napoleonic Wars by a Serving Officer.

BUGLER AND OFFICER OF THE RIFLES by William Green & Harry Smith—With the 95th (Rifles) during the Peninsular & Waterloo Campaigns of the Napoleonic Wars.

NAPOLEONIC WAR STORIES by Sir Arthur Quiller-Couch—Tales of soldiers, spies, battles & sieges from the Peninsular & Waterloo campaingns.

CAPTAIN OF THE 95TH (RIFLES) by Jonathan Leach—An officer of Wellington's sharpshooters during the Peninsular, South of France and Waterloo campaigns of the Napoleonic wars.

RIFLEMAN COSTELLO by Edward Costello—The adventures of a soldier of the 95th (Rifles) in the Peninsular & Waterloo Campaigns of the Napoleonic wars.

AVAILABLE ONLINE AT **www.leonaur.com**
AND FROM ALL GOOD BOOK STORES

www.ingramcontent.com/pod-product-compliance
Lightning Source LLC
Chambersburg PA
CBHW021003090426
42738CB00007B/628